British Game Birds and Waterfowl

by Beverly R. Morris
Revised by W.B. Tegetmeir

with an introduction by Jackson Chambers

This work contains material that was originally published in 1897.

This publication is within the Public Domain.

This edition is reprinted for educational purposes
and in accordance with all applicable Federal Laws.

Introduction Copyright 2018 by Jackson Chambers

Self Reliance Books

Get more historic titles on animal and stock breeding, gardening and old fashioned skills by visiting us at:

http://selfreliancebooks.blogspot.com/

Introduction

I am pleased to present yet another title on Raising Quail.

This volume is entitled "Quailology" and was published by Fred Kerr in 1903.

The work is in the Public Domain and is re-printed here in accordance with Federal Laws.

As with all reprinted books of this age that are intended to perfectly reproduce the original edition, considerable pains and effort had to be undertaken to correct fading and sometimes outright damage to existing proofs of this title. At times, this task is quite monumental, requiring an almost total "rebuilding" of some pages from digital proofs of multiple copies. Despite this, imperfections still sometimes exist in the final proof and may detract from the visual appearance of the text.

I hope you enjoy reading this book as much as I enjoyed making it available to readers again.

Jackson Chambers

PREFACE

THE popularity of Dr. Beverley Morris' "British Game
Birds and Wildfowl" is evidenced by the fact that the
work has passed through three large editions since its first
publication in 1855. Since that date, however, a vast fund
of information has been acquired respecting the history of
British Birds, more especially as regards the habits, nesting,
&c., of those of a migratory character. The investigations
in far-distant lands of such practical ornithologists as Lord
Lilford, Professor A. Newton, Canon Tristram, Mr. H.
Seebohm, Mr. Howard Saunders, Mr. Harvie-Brown, Mr.
Abel Chapman, Mr. Dresser, and many others, the results
of whose labours have been published subsequently to the
first issue of this work, have rendered it desirable that the
present edition should be revised—a labour which the pub-
lisher has requested me to undertake. In so doing I have
not attempted to alter the character of the work, or to rewrite
articles, on which the public has set the seal of its approba-
tion; but I have corrected many statements which have been
proved to be erroneous since they were first published, have
added much additional information more recently acquired,
and have endeavoured to bring the work up to date, by
reference to the voluminous works of Dresser ("Birds of
Europe"), Lord Lilford ("Illustrations of British Birds"),
Professor A. Newton and Howard Saunders ("Yarrell's

PREFACE

British Birds," 4th edition), Seebohm (" British Birds "), Booth (" Rough Notes "), and numerous local faunas, such as those of Macpherson, D'Urban and Mathew, Gray, Borrer, Harvie-Brown, &c.

The sixty hand-coloured plates have been carefully revised under my supervision.

Amongst the additions, I have added the vernacular names of the species in the different European countries, for which I am in great part indebted to Dresser. These names have been carefully indexed, so that the description of the birds to which they apply can be referred to without difficulty; and I have also appended to each article the names of a few of the books that may be advantageously consulted by those desirous of fuller information regarding the species described, which list has no pretension to be regarded as a complete Bibliography.

I trust that the alterations that have been effected in the form and substance of the work may render this old favourite more acceptable to the public.

W. B. TEGETMEIER.

North Finchley, N.
1895.

CONTENTS

VOLUME THE FIRST

BRITISH
GAME BIRDS AND WILDFOWL

THE PHEASANT

Phasianus colchicus, . . . Linnæus.

Phāsiănus, from the river Phasis in Colchis, whence it was said to
have been brought by the Argonautic expedition.
Colchĭcus, belonging to *Colchis*, a province of Asia east of the Black
Sea, now Mingrelia.

Faisan, French; *Fagiano*, Italian; *Edelfasan*, German.

WHETHER we look upon this very fine bird as an
ornament to our parks and woods, or in the more
gross and epicurean light of an additional luxury for our
tables, we cannot but consider the time of its introduction
into this country, upwards of seven hundred years ago, as a
very important epoch in the annals of the sportsman. In
Dugdale's "Monasticon Anglicanum" is a reference by
which it appears that the Abbot of Amesbury obtained a
licence to kill Hares and Pheasants in the first years of the
reign of King Henry I., which commenced on the 2nd
of August 1100; and Daniell, in his "Rural Sports," quotes
"Echard's History of England," to the effect that in the
year 1299 (the twenty-seventh of Edward I.) the price of a
Pheasant was fourpence, a couple of Woodcocks three-halfpence, a Mallard three-halfpence, and a Plover one penny.

To these notices might have been added another which seems to set the Pheasant at a higher premium—to wit, that in 1179 Thomas à Becket, on the day of his martyrdom, dined on a Pheasant, and enjoyed it, as it would seem from the remark of one of his monks that 'he dined more heartily and cheerfully that day than usual.' Those who are interested in the history of this mediæval bird will find a most interesting series of extracts respecting it in Mr. Harting's "Ornithology of Shakespeare." Its hardy nature, the readiness with which it breeds, and its rapid increase under favourable circumstances, have led to its introduction into all our preserves ; while its large size and peculiar habits have made it a very favourite object of pursuit to the poacher.

The original *locus a quo* of the Pheasant is generally believed to have been the banks of the river Phasis, now called Rion, which ran through the ancient Colchis, in Asia Minor. We thus find the origin of both the generic and specific names accounted for ; and although such an application of the names of places to designate this bird, would reasonably lead to the supposition that it had only, or at any rate chiefly, been originally an inhabitant of that particular district, yet such an idea is hardly reconcilable with its known hardiness, and the readiness with which it multiplies. But, however interesting it might be to pursue the subject of its general distribution over Europe and Asia, we must now confine ourselves to its consideration as a naturalised inhabitant of Great Britain and Ireland.

The natural habits of the Pheasant leading it, as they do, to frequent woods and copses, where some of its food is procured, and shelter obtained, there is now scarcely a district in these countries, where such shelter and moderate protection are afforded to it, where it is not to be found more or less abundantly. In Scotland, they are to be seen in greater or less numbers as far north as Sutherlandshire ; and in Ireland, although not so generally distributed as in England, they are by no means uncommon, having dispersed

themselves widely in the neighbourhood of the preserves
into which they have been introduced. But although the
Pheasant is thus widely distributed, and increases so rapidly,
there can be little doubt that its present existence in this
country, in a comparatively wild state, is to be attributed to
the care and attention bestowed by our noblemen and country
gentlemen upon its preservation, rather than upon the habits
of the bird in avoiding or eluding danger or destruction. So
large a bird, and one in such general esteem, both for the
beauty of its plumage and its excellence as an addition to
the luxuries of the table, is, as may naturally be expected,
eagerly sought after, both by those who desire it as an
ornament to their collections, and also by those who supply
the larders of the wealthy and luxurious.

Although the present custom of country gentlemen supplying the regular dealers with ample quantities of game
from their preserves, must greatly tend to diminish the
profits of the poacher, still the high price which is paid by
the dealers leaves a wide margin from which the illegal
sportsman may and does reap a very abundant harvest.

The most favourite resort of the Pheasant is the thick,
brushy underwood, composed of small shrubs, bramble
bushes, long coarse grass, and other wild plants, which is
often met with through the whole of small woods and
coppices, and in the outskirts of larger woods, or where
woods have been cut down and the brushwood allowed to
grow as it would. In such situations as the above the
Pheasant remains quiet and concealed during the day-time,
but at sunset and sunrise it leaves this seclusion for the
more open feeding-ground; it is singular that on these
occasions it never walks, but, we believe, invariably runs
from the cover to the place where it is accustomed to feed.
Its habitually frequenting the same cover and feeding-
ground leads to the formation of narrow runs or paths,
which, to the practised eye, tell with certainty the number
and kind of game to be expected. It is mentioned in
Thompson's " Natural History of Ireland," that in that

country Pheasants are frequently found during the summer and autumn months in the potato fields. We never remember to have noticed the Pheasant in such a locality in England ; but the extensive culture of the potato in Ireland, may account for this adaptation of its habits to the necessities of the case.

During the autumn, winter, and early spring months the Pheasant perches in trees when at roost ; but from the beginning of April till the middle or end of September its roosting-place is among the long and coarse grass and sedge of its favourite cover. On withdrawing from the trees as roosting-places in the spring, the Hen bird is the first to set the example ; but the Cock Pheasant does not abandon his tree for several weeks later. When, however, they have taken to the ground, they do not again use the trees at night, unless something has occurred to disturb them. During the winter single individuals will frequently leave the coverts ; and, if not molested, will remain for a considerable time at a distance from their natural haunts, and during this period they usually roost in hedges, or thick grass or stubble, seldom resorting to trees as roosting-places. These stragglers are the exceptions ; as a common rule, Pheasants will be found in winter roosting in trees, and generally somewhat in company—where one is found, others may be expected at no great distance. The tree preferred by the Pheasant for its nocturnal resting-place is the larch fir when attainable ; and this probably arises from the peculiar growth of this tree—the branches being nearly at right-angles to the trunk. Their preference for these trees, which are partially denuded of their leaves in the winter, gives additional facilities to the poacher for their destruction, as so large a bird is very readily seen on the almost naked branches, and offers an easy mark to his gun.

When undisturbed, this bird will not unfrequently associate with the barn-door fowl around the farm-yard ; and we have known many instances of their roosting among trees within a very short distance of the house ; but in such cases a gun was never discharged anywhere near their haunts. Still, although the Pheasant courts our protection, and will readily become tolerably familiar, it cannot be brought into a completely domestic state. On this point the opinion of Charles Waterton will be considered decisive :—" Notwithstanding the proximity of the Pheasant to the nature of the barn-door fowl, still it has that within it which baffles every attempt on our part to render its domestication complete. What I allude to is, a most singular innate timidity which never fails to show itself on the sudden and abrupt appearance of an object ; I spent some months in trying to overcome this timorous propensity in the Pheasant, but I failed completely in the attempt. The young birds which had been hatched under a domestic hen soon became very tame, and would even receive food from the hand when it was offered cautiously to them ; they would fly up to the window, and would feed in company with the common poultry ; but if anybody approached them unawares, off they went to the nearest cover, with surprising velocity ; they remained in it till all was quiet, and then returned with their usual confidence. Two of them lost their lives in the water, by the unexpected appearance of a pointer ; while the barn-door fowls seemed scarcely to notice the presence of the intruder. The rest took finally to the woods at the commencement of the breeding season. This particular kind of timidity, which does not appear in our domestic fowls, seems to me to oppose the only, though at the same time an insurmountable, bar to our final triumph over the Pheasant. After attentive observation, I can perceive nothing else in the habits of the bird to serve as a clue by which we may be enabled to trace the cause of failure in the many attempts which have been made to invite it to breed in our yards, and retire to rest with the barn-door fowl and turkey."

We have never known any one succeed to the extent Mr. Waterton did, at Walton, though it is not uncommon for those that have been brought up by the domestic hen to come regularly to be fed when called ; but their numbers will gradually diminish either by desertion or destruction, till those that are left take to the woods at the beginning of the breeding-season.

The crowing of the Pheasant, resembling the imperfect attempt of a young fowl, is continued the whole year at the time of roosting; it is frequently heard through the night, and again at sunrise; and during the hours of daylight it will often crow on the occurrence of any sudden disturbance or noise, such as a gunshot or peal of thunder. It is remarkable that it is followed, and not preceded, as in the Game-Cock, by the clapping of the wings, the Pheasant and the domestic Cock invariably reversing the order of the succession of these two actions.

The possession of habits such as we have detailed, cannot fail to render the Pheasant an easy prey to the poacher; and we will now describe the various modes in which this bird is feloniously abstracted from its native preserves. The most usual and deadly method of destruction is undoubtedly by the fowling-piece; and various are the changes and alterations which this weapon undergoes to enable the poacher to carry it without detection to the scene of his labours. We have now before our mind's eye a particularly curious instrument of this kind, which was taken, along with its owner, on the manor of a friend of ours, where it had just killed a fine Cock Pheasant; it and he were taken indeed *flagrante delicto*. The gun consisted of a stock of the smallest and rudest home manufacture, quite capable of concealment in the coat pocket; a large old-fashioned flint musket-lock was roughly attached to it, and it was fitted with a small short barrel, composed of a piece of thin iron tubing, about six inches long, soldered on to the barrel of an ancient horse-pistol, making altogether a tube of some seventeen or eighteen inches in length. To all appearance it would have been much more likely to carry death or injury to its owner than to any-thing at which it was aimed, and yet it was used effectively, certainly on one occasion. We have seen other poaching guns, but never another at all comparable to this one for rudeness and apparent danger. The time chosen by the poacher for shooting the Pheasant is usually after it has retired to roost for the night. It is not often that the Pheasant-poacher goes out alone, for he is well aware that on the first sound of his gun he will have the keepers upon him, and in that case he must beat a retreat, or be taken ; his more usual plan is to join with a number of other similarly-intentioned people with himself, and then take the covers by storm ; and if the keepers come in contact with them, a general fight ensues, which too often ends in bloodshed.

Another very destructive method of poaching, and which is always carried on by a single person, is the setting silk or wire snares in the runs of the Pheasants. These are set quietly during the day, and are generally allowed to remain till the feeding-time of the birds, when, on running with their heads stretched forward, as is their custom, they are caught in the snickles or nooses, and the poacher, watching his opportunity, quietly removes his snares and his victims. Sometimes, however, having set his snares, he proceeds to drive the Pheasants in the cover by the aid of a silent cur dog. Having thus driven the birds into his snares, he at once collects the plunder, and hides it, to be removed at nightfall.

Pheasants are also said to be sometimes caused to fall into the poacher's hands by being fumigated to stupefaction or suffocation while on their perches asleep. Mr. Waterton, a high authority on these subjects, considers this an idle story, and says that, though he has repeatedly tried the plan, he never could succeed in bringing one bird down from its roost.

Having now given a slight outline of the usual stratagems had recourse to by poachers in the pursuit of the Pheasant, we are led naturally to consider the best methods by which we may baffle them, and secure for our own use the birds we have been at so much trouble and expense in preserving. We should endeavour to turn to our own advantage the natural habits of the bird, but which, under ordinary circumstances, render it an easy prey to the poacher. No one has written more to the purpose on this point, or with more accurate knowledge of the habits of the bird, than Charles Waterton, and we cannot, therefore, do better than give, in his own words, his admirable hints on the best method of securing our game from the arts of the poacher :—

"In order to render useless all attempts of the nocturnal poacher to destroy the Pheasants, it is absolutely necessary that a place of security should be formed. I know of no position more appropriate than a piece of level ground, at the bottom of a hill, bordered by a gentle stream. About three acres of this, sowed with whins, and surrounded by a holly fence, to keep the cattle out, would be the very thing. In the centre of it, for the space of one acre, there ought to be planted spruce fir trees, about fourteen feet asunder. Next to the larch, this species of tree is generally preferred by the Pheasants for their roosting-place ; and it is quite impossible that the poachers can shoot them in these trees. Moreover Magpies and Jays will always resort to them at night-fall ; and they never fail to give the alarm on the first appearance of an enemy. Many a time has the Magpie been of essential service to me in a night excursion after poachers. If there be no park wall, an eye ought to be kept, from time to time, on the neighbouring hedges. Poachers are apt to set horse-hair snares in them ; and these villainous nooses give the Pheasants apoplexy. Six or seven dozen of wooden Pheasants, nailed on the branches of trees in the surrounding woods, cause unutterable vexation and loss of ammunition to these amateurs of nocturnal plunder. Small clumps of hollies, and yew trees with holly hedges round them, are of infinite service, when planted at intervals of one hundred and fifty yards. To these the Pheasants fly on the sudden approach of danger during the day, and skulk there till the alarm is over." "If to these arrangements for protecting Pheasants, there could be added a park wall, from nine to ten feet high, and inclosing about two hundred and fifty acres, consisting of wood, meadow, pasture, and arable land, the naturalist might put all enemies at defiance, and revel in the enchanting scene afforded by the different evolutions of single pairs and congregated groups of animated nature."

We are convinced that if the principles laid down in these remarks were generally considered and acted upon by our large landed proprietors the poacher would have but a sorry chance of ever securing more than a stray bird, which would never be missed; and we cannot but think also that, by thus calling in the aid of Nature, we should very materially diminish the present enormous expense which attends the preservation of the Pheasant. The expense of preserving game must necessarily vary considerably from a variety of local causes, and it would be difficult, probably, to average it; but we have heard a large landed proprietor assert that every head of game, including in the list, Pheasants, Partridges, and Hares, cost him at least ten shillings. This, probably, was rather an extreme but certainly not an exceptional case; for we have heard the same amount estimated in other widely distant localities.

It is well known that birds which have been snared will keep longer than those which have been shot, and the dealers will in consequence pay more for them; this should be an additional reason for reducing the cost of game, in the legitimate way, to the dealers, so as to render all competition by the poacher out of the question.

The food of the Pheasant is of a very miscellaneous character; and although it is commonly considered that it inflicts injury upon the farmer, by the quantity of wheat, oats, barley, beans, and peas which it consumes, yet it must be admitted that, whatever positive injury it commits, it also does so large an amount of good to the farmer that it may be fair matter for consideration and experiment, whether the good does not considerably outweigh the evil, where the birds are not permitted to increase beyond what reason and experience would point out as the proper limit to their numbers.

The food of the Pheasant varies considerably, according to the season of the year; in the autumn and winter its chief subsistence is derived from seeds of various kinds, such as acorns, of which it is very fond, hazel nuts, beech mast, haws, or the fruit of the whitethorn, hips, the seed-vessels of the wild roses, wheat, oats, barley, beans, peas, buckwheat, and a long catalogue of seeds of wild plants, many of them very injurious to the farmer, but 'quæ nunc describere longum;' in addition to these it consumes, especially during the summer and autumnal months, a very considerable quantity of insects, which, if allowed to multiply, would do much damage to the crops.

In the spring and summer its food consists chiefly of roots of various kinds, some succulent plants, and an innumerable host of insects of all sorts. Among the roots on which it feeds at this time of the year, may be mentioned those of 'Potentilla anserina,' 'Ranunculus bulbosus,' the garden tulip, to which it is said to be extremely partial, and those of numerous other plants. The root of the Jerusalem artichoke is also a favourite, and the potato, particularly when boiled. Among the succulent plants may be named the young shoots of clover, young twigs of trees, grass, and the tubers of 'Ranunculus ficaria,' one of our earliest flowering spring buttercups. Mr. Watters, in his work on the "Birds of Ireland," says that on one occasion he found a field-mouse in the crop of a Pheasant; and several instances of their swallowing Slow-worms (Anguis fragilis) and young vipers are on record. To the above catalogue may be added the leaves and bulbs of the turnip, but only occasionally. Mr. Waterton recommends as a valuable addition to a pheasantry, the planting a few roods with the thousand-headed cabbage; the seeds sown in April, and the young plants transplanted in June, two feet asunder. These afford very excellent food for the birds during the late autumn and winter, and are particularly useful when the ground is deeply covered with snow. This alone, however, is not a sufficient provision for the winter, and it becomes necessary, in order to prevent them from straying abroad in search of food, to supply them with it in the coverts. Beans and boiled potatoes are strongly recommended by Mr. Waterton as being far cheaper than oats or barley, much of which is devoured by Sparrows and other small birds. The food should be placed under yew trees, holly bushes, or the spruce fir, and it will then escape the Ring Dove and Rook.

Mr. Yarrell suggests that it is a good plan "to sow in summer, beans, peas, and buckwheat mixed together, leaving the whole crop standing on the ground; the strong and tall stalks of the beans carry up, sustain, and support the other two, and all three afford together, for a long time, both food and cover."

Like other gallinaceous birds, the Pheasant always swallows a number of small stones, which enable the gizzard to grind up the food into a uniform pulpy mass, which is then readily digested.

In sporting phraseology the terms applied to Pheasants are the following :—Two Pheasants are a 'Brace;' three a 'Leash.' The brood is called a 'Ni,' 'Nid,' or 'Nide,' from the Latin *nidus*, a nest. In putting Pheasants up you are said to 'Push' or 'Spring' them.

The time for Pheasant-shooting is fixed by law to commence on the first of October; but it very frequently happens that the birds are then scarcely sufficiently grown, and this has induced many preservers of game to keep their preserves closed till a later day, sometimes even till the first of November. By this forbearance they not only secure finer birds, but also much more agreeable shooting; for by that time many of the trees will have lost much of their leafy covering, and consequently there will be less obstruction to the use of the gun. The shooting ends on the first of February.

During the day, particularly early in the season, Pheasants lie very close, and will almost allow you to walk over them; it is therefore absolutely necessary to beat every inch of the cover. This was formerly done by spaniels, which for this purpose should be slow, short-legged animals, which do their work quietly, and keep within reach of you. Many sportsmen, however, prefer trusting the disturbance of the Pheasants to men, who, by beating the bushes and thickets, effectually drive out the birds. This can hardly fail to ensure good sport, if there is any game in the cover In this case a retriever is of course necessary to find the dead and wounded birds. In Pheasant-shooting, the hen birds, which are easily known by the shortness of the tail, are generally allowed to escape.

Having carefully gone over the covers, it will be advisable to examine and beat the hedgerows near them, for many of the Pheasants, on being disturbed in their cover, will run to them for shelter, and will afford by far the best shots.

Should the coverts be very wet, the birds will not remain in them, but take to the hedgerows near for shelter. It is therefore desirable on such occasions to commence with the hedgerows, and by keeping between the Pheasants and the cover, so as to cut them off from their places of security, you may be sure of some good sport.

When the young sportsman has got over the nervous feeling, which is very generally caused by the sudden whirr and rush of the Pheasant on rising, he will find it a bird easily shot, as from its large size and steady flight it offers a good mark to aim at. The time to fire is when it has finished its spiral-mounting flight on first rising, and just as it begins to make right away. The head should be aimed at, as the bird is thus less injured for the table than if shot in any other part of the body. The quality of coolness and steadiness cannot be too much cultivated by the young shooter, and in Pheasant - shooting this is doubly necessary.

The Pheasant is, *par excellence*, the game chosen for battue shooting. Where birds are very plentiful, and have been kept unmolested for a particular day, when the cover is besieged with a large party of shooters, keepers, and beaters, the numbers shot by individuals are often very great.

The nest of the Pheasant is of a very simple kind, and is composed of dry grass and leaves; it is usually placed in woods in some clump of thick brush or underwood, or in a tuft of the long coarse grass so often found in such situations; clover fields are, however, not uncommonly selected, and afford good shelter.   The number of eggs varies from eight or ten to fourteen, and occasionally even as many as sixteen or eighteen.

In preserves, nests will nevertheless sometimes be found with an unusual number of eggs; these are generally considered to result from more than one Hen Pheasant laying in the same nest. This is the more probable, as the eggs of wild birds have occasionally been found deposited in the nest of one of a different species; and Pheasants, Partridges, and even fowls occasionally have a nest in common.

The eggs of the Pheasant are in length about one inch and three-quarters by about one inch and a half in breadth; they are of one uniform colour, a very pretty olive-brown, which has a particularly chaste and pleasant effect.

The natural instinct of self-preservation guides the Pheasant to avoid, as much as possible, running to its place of concealment, which would necessarily leave a track as well as scent.   It will accordingly very generally, on ending its flight, drop suddenly into the spot it has chosen for its hiding-place; and this is more particularly the case with the female when sitting.

The Hen Pheasant, when leaving her nest voluntarily, covers her eggs with leaves.   When disturbed, however, this is of course omitted; but on these occasions she leaves the nest with extreme reluctance, and we have on several occasions seen her almost allow herself to be caught by the hand before she would take to flight.   The young birds are hatched from the end of May to the beginning of July, and remain under the mother's protection till the end of August, or early in September, when they commence moulting, and finally assume the adult plumage, having completed this by about the middle of October.

The eggs of the Pheasant are hatched in large numbers by domestic poultry, many thousands being reared under Hens on large estates. This method of rearing young Pheasants is also followed where the eggs have been exposed in mowing, or are deposited so near any thoroughfare as to endanger their being found. Young Pheasants that have been hatched in this way, as we may say artificially, require to be supplied plentifully with insect food, such as ants' eggs, of which they are very fond, woodlice, earwigs, beetles, and grubs of all kinds. We have seen boiled vermicelli recommended, but cannot speak from experience as to its fitness or otherwise. Young Pheasants when first hatched are covered with a soft down, and are able at once to run about and feed themselves. Female Pheasants, when confined in runs for the supply of eggs, rarely become broody.

The Pheasant is subject, like the common fowl and other gallinaceous birds, to the presence of the gape-worm (*Sclerostoma syngamus*) in the trachea or wind-pipe, and which produces death from suffocation and swelling of the lining membrane, by the little animal, which adheres to the surface by a sucker. The disease caused by the 'Sclerostoma' is commonly called the Gapes, and chiefly attacks the young birds. There is no very effectual remedy when the birds are once affected; but its recurrence is easily prevented by rearing the young birds on fresh soil, as is always done by intelligent keepers.

The occurrence of female Pheasants in a plumage very nearly resembling that of the male is by no means uncommon. The tail increases in length, the scarlet skin round the eye is developed, and the plumage generally assumes more or less that of the male bird. In these cases the change seems to depend upon a diseased condition of the ovaries; for none exhibiting this curious change of plumage have ever been known to breed. One which was bred on the estate of a friend of ours, and was remarkably tame and familiar, assumed this plumage at the age, we believe, of thirteen years. Similar changes occur occasionally in domestic poultry, in the Peafowl, and even in the domestic Duck.

In addition to the Pheasant first introduced into this country from Asia Minor, various other species have been brought to this country and are now denizens of our woods and covers. Of these the most common is the Chinese ring-necked Pheasant (*P. torquatus*). This has been so widely spread that pure Colchian Pheasants are rare, almost all specimens showing a patch of white upon the neck. Another very beautiful Pheasant has been obtained from Japan, the *P. versicolor*. This also breeds freely with the common and the ring-necked Pheasant, and their offspring are perfectly fertile. On the Continent of Asia numerous other sub-species exist, such as the white-winged Pheasant (*P. principalis*), the Mongolian Pheasant, &c. It is remarkable that all species of the true Pheasants breed freely together, and produce perfectly fertile offspring, so that it is difficult to get in this country a pure specimen of any one of the species. Variations in the colour of the Pheasant also constantly occur; thus we have Pheasants purely white, and others pied with white; another variety of pale buff colour is called the Bohemian Pheasant.

Hybrid Pheasants are not very rare, but they are always unproductive; the cross with the domestic fowl is not uncommon; and instances are on record in which the Pheasant has paired with the Black Grouse and other species.

The Pheasant is certainly polygamous, and when the male bird has selected his 'beat,' he commences clapping his wings and crowing, which is a defiance to any other male birds that may hear it, as well as a call note for the females; before, however, he can consider himself the lord and master of the latter, he must conquer and expel from his territory all of his own sex. For this purpose he is provided, as are the males of all polygamous animals, with lethal weapons—the spurs with which to kill or drive away his rivals. The distinction is well seen in gallinaceous birds.

The Partridge and Grouse pair, and are consequently spurless; the Pheasant and Jungle Fowl are polygamous and are spurred.

At the beginning of the breeding season the cheeks of the Cock Pheasant assume a brighter scarlet; in displaying his plumage to the Hens, he drops the wing next to them, and turns the tail, so as to display the upper surface.

The Plumage of the Pheasant varies with the species which chiefly predominates in its ancestry; but it may be generally described as follows:—The adult Cock Pheasant has the bill of a light horn colour; darker at the base. Irides, yellow hazel. The eyes are surrounded by a naked papillose skin, of a very bright scarlet colour, minutely dotted over with black specks; under each eye is a small patch of feathers of a dark spotted glossy purple. Crown of head, bronzed green, the feathers somewhat elongated; on each side of occiput is a tuft of dark golden-green feathers, erectible at pleasure;— very conspicuous in the pairing season. The rest of the head and upper part of the neck, deep purple, brown, green, or blue, as seen in different lights; lower part of neck and breast, reddish chestnut, each feather with a black margin; lower part of breast and sides the same, each feather largely tipped with black, reflecting glossy purple. Feathers of upper part of back, orange-red, tipped with black; feathers of back and scapulars have the centre black, or spotted with black, outside which is a yellowish band, and the outer margin red-orange. Lower part of back and tail coverts, purplish red, tinged with green, purple, and other reflections—the feathers long and pendent; quill feathers, dull greyish brown, varied with pale wood brown; wing coverts, of two shades of red; centre of belly, thighs, vent, and under tail coverts brownish black. Tail feathers, very long, the two middle ones the longest, occasionally measuring two feet; the outside ones, which are the shortest, are less than six inches long; all are of a reddish brown with transverse lines of black, about one inch apart. Legs, toes, and claws, dusky; on each leg is a spur, which becomes sharp after the first year.

The female is less than the male; the whole plumage more

sober; general colour light brown, varied with darker brown and black; the upper part of the neck in some lights shows iridescent reflections; space round the eye is feathered; breast and belly, dotted with small black spots on a light ground. Tail, shorter than, but barred similarly to, that of the male.

Young birds resemble the female in plumage.

In weight the Cock Pheasant will commonly attain to about two pounds and a half; but Mr. Yarrell gives several instances in which, from the abundance of food in the preserves, they had attained the enormous weight of four pounds and a half. Mr. Tegetmeier states that he weighed one male of the common species that turned the scale at five pounds, and even greater weights have been recorded.

The Cock Pheasant measures in length nearly three feet; the female measures only two feet, owing to the comparative shortness of her tail, and its somewhat smaller size.

The culinary value of the Pheasant is well known. The different species now common in Great Britain, namely, the Colchian, the Chinese, and the Japanese, do not appear to differ in value for the table, but young hen birds of the year are most esteemed.

BIBLIOGRAPHY.

ELLIOT's " Monograph of the Phasianidæ."—This magnificent folio contains coloured plates by Wolf of all the various species of Pheasants known at the date of publication. It was published by subscription. Copies are now scarce, and usually realise about £40 when on sale.

TEGETMEIER on " Pheasants."—Contains the most complete account of the various Pheasants reared in England, with very full details of their habits and management.

DRESSER, " Birds of Europe," Vol. VII.—Contains a detailed account of the distribution of the 'P. colchicus' in Europe. The common species is now so generally crossed with the ring-necked and Japanese, that the author had to procure specimens from Asia Minor to secure an accurate representation.

THE CAPERCAILLIE

COCK OF THE WOODS—WOOD GROUSE.

Tetrao urogallus, ... Linnæus.

Tetrao, a bird mentioned by Pliny.
Urogallus from *Urus,* a wild ox, and *Gallus,* a Cock.

Coq de bruyère, French; *Auerhahn,* German; *Tiur,* Norwegian;
Tjäder, Swedish; *Glouhar,* Russian; *Capult-coille,* Gaelic.

THIS magnificent and lordly bird was, when Great Britain and Ireland were more heavily timbered than at the present day, an abundant inhabitant of both countries, and although, as the inhabitants increased, and the wood diminished, it gradually became more and more rare, till at length the breed became extinct; in Ireland, somewhere about 1760, till which date it lingered in the woods of Tipperary; and in Scotland, about the year 1780, when the last was killed near Inverness. But its very judicious and spirited introduction into their woods, by some of our largest landed proprietors, which has of late years taken place, has been most successful, and its very peculiar cry may again be heard in many extensive plantations.

The history of its recent reintroduction into these islands is one of much interest. The first attempt at again introducing this fine bird into this country was made in the end of 1827, or beginning of 1828, by Lord Fyfe. One pair was brought from Sweden, and the attempt was made at Mar Lodge to naturalise them; it, however, failed, owing to the death of the hen bird immediately on her arrival in the country. The male bird paired with a barn-door fowl in

1828, and one hybrid chicken was produced, but was found dead soon after its exclusion from the egg. In January 1829 another pair was imported, and in April the hen commenced laying, and laid altogether about two dozen eggs. Many of these she broke and ate, but eight were secured, and placed under a common Hen ; but one bird was produced, and it soon died. The next year the Hen Capercaillie laid eight eggs ; one of these she broke, and sat on the others for five weeks, but they were all addled.

The year following, 1831, other eggs were produced, two of which were hatched by the mother, and four by a common Hen. The time of incubation in both instances was twenty-nine days. Of these six but two survived, after a few weeks. It does not appear, however, that the experiment was altogether a successful one, though sufficiently so to induce renewed endeavours to effect the wished-for object.

In July 1837 twenty-eight Capercaillies were presented to the Marquis of Breadalbane, by Mr. Thomas Fowell Buxton, who had procured them from Sweden direct, by the exertions of Mr. Lloyd, whose admirable work on the " Field Sports of Norway and Sweden" contains much and valuable information on the habits of this bird. Mr. Buxton sent over his Irish gamekeeper, Lawrence Banville, with Mr. Lloyd, to Sweden, that he might take charge of the birds collected, and bring them to Taymouth Castle, the seat of the Marquis of Breadalbane.

In the autumn of 1837 some of these birds were turned out into the woods, the others being kept in confinement. In 1838 the keeper reared one brace, and two fine broods were produced in the woods. This summer sixteen more hens were imported, making altogether thirteen cocks and twenty-nine hens. The experiment of rearing by hand does not appear to have been very successful, and led to the more effective method of placing the Capercaillie's eggs, produced in confinement, under the Gray Hen, or female Black Grouse. This plan seems to have answered remarkably well, and numerous fine broods, of eight or ten each, have been the result. Several broods were also produced by the Capercaillie that had been turned out, thus placing beyond the possibility of doubt, the fact that, with proper care and attention, these birds may be induced to breed in our larger woods and preserves. The ultimate effect of this well-devised and admirably-conducted experiment has been most successful, and has met with an admirable historian in the person of Mr. Harvie-Brown, who gives the fullest details in his work on the " Capercaillie in Scotland." Certainly the climate is not likely to interfere with its complete naturalisation, for we find it inhabiting Norway, Sweden, Northern Russia—both in Europe and Asia—Germany, Hungary, and some parts of the Alps. In fact, wherever very extensive pine forests afford it food and shelter, there it is found in more or less abundance.

The favourite haunts of the Cock of the Woods are extensive pine forests; in these it usually remains during the whole year, and is seldom or never found in coppices or small cover. Some, however, occasionally breed on the sides of the lofty mountains, but as the cold increases, and deep snow lies on the ground, they generally betake themselves to the lower and more sheltered grounds. " Excepting there be a deep snow, the Capercaillie is much upon the ground in the daytime; very commonly, however, he sits on the pines." During the night he usually roosts in the trees; but if the weather is very severe, he buries himself in the snow for warmth and shelter. Mr. Lloyd says that the flight of the Capercaillie is not heavy for so large a bird; and that the noise it makes during flight is not greater than you would expect from a bird of its dimensions. Although this bird usually takes but short flights, he will, on some occasions, rise to a considerable height in the air, and take a flight of several miles at a time. As before stated, the Capercaillie perches much in the pines, and will most frequently be found in the winter sitting on the highest branches of these trees.

"Even in his wild state, the Capercaillie occasionally forgets his inherent shyness, and will attack people when approaching his place of resort. Mr. Alderberg mentions such an occurrence:—During a number of years an old Capercaillie Cock had been in the habit of frequenting the estate of Villinge, at Wermdö, who, as often as he heard the voice of people in the adjoining wood, had the boldness to station himself on the ground, and during a continual flapping of his wings, pecked at the legs and feet of those that disturbed his domain.

"Mr. Brehm, also, mentionsa Capercaillie Cock that frequented a wood a mile distant from Renthendorf, in which was a path or roadway. The bird, as soon as it perceived any person approach, would fly towards him, peck at his legs, and rap him with his wings, and was with difficulty driven away. A huntsman succeeded in taking this bird, and carried it to a place two miles (about fourteen English) distant; but on the following day the Capercaillie resumed its usual haunt. Another person afterwards caught him, with a view of carrying him to the Ofwer-Jägmästare. At first the bird remained quiet, but he soon began to tear and peck at the man so effectually that the latter was compelled to restore him to his liberty. However, after the lapse of a few months, he totally disappeared, probably having fallen into the hands of a less timid bird catcher."

Early in the season, if the Capercaillie is disturbed by a dog, it seldom flies far, and soon perches again. Later in the season they become excessively wild, especially the cocks. "Towards the commencement of, and during the continuance of winter, the Capercaillies are generally in packs; these, which are usually composed wholly of cocks (the hens keeping apart), do not separate until the approach of spring. These packs, which are said sometimes to contain fifty or a hundred birds, usually hold to the sides of the numerous lakes and morasses, with which the northern forests abound; and to follow the same in the winter-time with a good rifle is no ignoble amusement."

When speaking of the habits of this bird during the period of incubation, Mr. Lloyd says, " At this period, and often when the ground is deeply covered with snow, the cock stations himself on a pine, and commences his love-song, or 'play,' as it is termed in Sweden, to attract the hens about him.   This is usually from the first dawn of day to sunrise, or from a little after sunset until it is quite dark. The time, however, more or less depends upon the mildness of the weather and the advanced state of the season.

"During his play, the neck of the Capercaillie is stretched out, his tail is raised, and spread like a fan, his wings droop, his feathers are ruffled up, and, in short, he much resembles in appearance an angry Turkey Cock.   He begins his play with a call something resembling 'Peller, peller, peller;' these sounds he repeats at first at some little intervals, but as he proceeds they increase in rapidity, until at last, and after perhaps the lapse of a minute or so, he makes a sort of 'gulp' in his throat, and finishes with sucking in, as it were, his breath.   During the continuance of this latter process, which only lasts a few seconds, the head of the Capercaillie is thrown up, his eyes are partially closed, and his whole appearance would denote that he is worked up into an agony of passion.   At this time his faculties are much absorbed, and it is not difficult to approach him; many, indeed, and among the rest Mr. Nilsson, assert that the Capercaillie can then neither see nor hear; and that he is not aware of the report or flash of a gun, even if fired immediately near to him.   To this assertion I cannot agree; for, though it is true that if the Capercaillie has not been much disturbed previously, he is not easily frightened during the last note, if so it may be termed, of his play; should the contrary be the case, he is constantly on the watch, and I have reason to know that, even at that time, if noise be made, or that a person exposes himself incautiously, he takes alarm, and immediately flies.

"The play of the Capercaillie is not loud; and should there be wind stirring in the trees at the time, it cannot be heard at any considerable distance. Indeed, during the calmer and most favourable weather, it is not audible at more than two or three hundred paces.

"On hearing the call of the cock, the hens, whose cry in some degree resembles the croak of the Raven, or rather, perhaps the sounds 'Gock, gock, gock,' assemble from all parts of the surrounding forest. The male bird now descends from the eminence on which he was perched, to the ground, where he and his female friends join company.

"The Capercaillie does not play indiscriminately over the forest; but he has his certain stations (Tjaderlek, which may perhaps be rendered his playing-ground); these, however, are often of some little extent. Here, unless very much persecuted, the song of these birds may be heard in the spring for years together. The Capercaillie does not, during his play, confine himself to any particular tree, for, on the contrary, it is seldom he is to be met with exactly on the same spot for two days in succession. On these 'lek' several Capercaillie may occasionally be heard playing at the same time; Mr. Greiff, in his quaint way, observes, 'it then goes gloriously.' But so long as the old male birds are alive, they will not, it is said, permit the young ones, or those of the preceding season, to play. Should the old birds, however, be killed, the young ones, in the course of a day or two, usually open their pipes. Combats, as it may be supposed, not unfrequently take place on these occasions; though I do not recollect having heard of more than two of these birds being engaged at the same time.

"The Capercaillie occasionally strikes up a few notes in the manner in which I have spoken, during the autumnal months — about Michaelmas, I believe. For this it is perhaps difficult to assign a reason. Mr. Greiff suggests, 'that it may be to show the young birds where the "lek" is situated.' I have never myself heard the Capercaillie playing at this period of the year; but I have met with men, on whose word I am inclined to place confidence, who have repeatedly killed them at that time, whilst so occupied.

"The Capercaillie lives to a considerable age; at least so I infer from the cocks not attaining their full growth until their third year or upward. The old ones may be easily known from their greater bulk, their Eagle-like bill, and the more beautiful glossiness of their plumage."

The Capercaillie is, as may be gathered from the above extracts, polygamous; and as soon as the hens begin to sit, they are deserted by the males, who skulk about among the brushwood, till their plumage is renewed.

With regard to the methods adopted for the capture of the Capercaillie, it is probable that somewhat similar devices are used to those so successful in the destruction of the Pheasant. In Norway and Sweden so different are the ideas of sporting to ours, that the regular sportsman there adopts measures for its capture, which we should here consider most unsportsman-like, and such as would only be used by the poacher. Custom, however, is everything, and there can be little doubt that the modes of capture we are now about to relate will frequently fill the game bag, when it would otherwise have returned empty. Mr. Lloyd says that "During the autumnal months, after flushing and dispersing the brood, people place themselves in ambush, and imitate the cry of the old or young birds, as circumstances may require. The manner in which this is practised may be better understood from what Mr. Greiff says on the subject :—

"'After the brood has been dispersed, and you see the growth they have acquired, the dogs are to be bound up, and a hut formed precisely on the spot from whence they were driven, in which you place yourself to call; and you adapt your call according to the greater or less size of the young birds. When they are as large as the hen, you ought not to begin to call until an hour after they have been flushed; should you wish to take them alive, a net is placed round him who calls. Towards the quarter the hen flies, there are seldom to be found any of the young birds, for she tries by her cackling to draw the dogs after her, and from her young ones. So long as you wish to continue your sport, you must not go out of your hut to collect the birds you have shot. When the hen answers the call, or lows like a cow, she has either got a young one with her, or the calling is incorrect; or else she has been frightened, and will not then quit her place. A young hen answers more readily to the call than an old one.'"

This must be a most destructive system, and would, we should think, almost lead to the annihilation of the game, if carried on to any extent. The following is Mr. Greiff's account of the various devices adopted in Scandinavia for the capture of the Capercaillie, and other birds of similar habits :—"Most of the forest birds are caught in the autumn by bird-lime, or the usual snares, and also by nets. In all these methods it is necessary to lead the bird by low rows of brushwood into small pathways; with snares of fine brass-wire suspended over these he is easily caught. One of my own methods, by which I have amused myself, and taken many birds alive, is by a simple knotted square silk net, of thirty inches width in the square, and the meshes so large that the Capercaillie can easily put his head through; this is to be hung over the pathway, and fastened slightly to small branches by weak woollen yarn, just sufficient to support the net in a square form, with some small twigs and leaves of the fir spread over it; round the net a silk line is passed through the extreme meshes, and fastened to a stout bush. When the Capercaillie has got his head into the mesh of the net, and finds that something opposes him, he always runs directly forward, when the silk line is drawn close, and the bird lies as if in a reticule, with his wings pressed to his body, unable to. move himself, or to tear the net, however weak it may be, although it should always be made of twisted silk. In the autumn, when the cranberry is plentiful in the forest, by strewing these berries on each side of the net, you entice the birds to advance eagerly. This sport produces much amusement. One night, when a sufficiency of snow fell to enable me to trace them, three

Wolves passed within ten paces of a Capercaillie, who had been caught in the net the night before; still the Wolves never injured the bird."

Other methods are also mentioned by Mr. Lloyd, by which a great destruction of the Capercaillie is effected. "In other instances the Capercaillie is shot in the night-time by torch-light. This plan, which is said to be very destructive, is, I believe, confined to the southern provinces of Sweden, for in the more northern parts of that country I never heard of its being adopted. In Smaland and Oster-göthland this is said to be effected in the following manner :— Towards night-fall people watch the last flight of the Caper-caillie before they go to roost. The direction they have taken into the forest is then carefully marked, by means of a prostrate tree, or by one which is felled especially for the purpose. After dark, two men start in pursuit of the birds; one of them is provided with a gun, the other with a long pole, to either end of which a flambeau is attached. The man with the flambeau goes in advance, the other remaining at the prostrate tree, to keep it and the two lights in an exact line with each other; by this curious contrivance they cannot well go astray in the forest. They thus proceed, occasionally halting, and taking a fresh mark, until they come near to the spot where they have reason to suppose the birds are roosting. They now carefully examine the trees, and when they discover the objects of their pursuit, which are said stupidly to remain gazing at the fire blazing beneath, they shoot them at their leisure. Should there be several Capercaillie in the same tree, however, it is always necessary to shoot those on the lower branches in the first instance; for, unless one of these birds falls on its companions, it is said the rest will never move, and, in consequence, the whole of them may be readily killed."

It appears, however, that the most destructive operations are carried on against the Capercaillie during the breeding-season. At this time the gunner, taking advantage of the complete abstraction of the cock bird when at his 'play,' approaches carefully, waiting always till the bird has nearly come to the end of his song, before venturing to move; he is, however, only able to advance a few steps—three or four— and must there remain like a statue, till the bird again arrives at the same point of his play, when another advance of a few feet is made, and so on till he is within easy shot. As might be expected, the Cock Capercaillie is generally the only sufferer on these occasions; were it otherwise, the breed would soon become extinct.

The food of the adult Capercaillie when wild appears to consist chiefly of the leaves of the Scotch fir (*Pinus sylvestris*), or Tal, as it is termed in Sweden; while the leaves of the common spruce fir (*Abies excelsa*), called Gran in Sweden, are but very rarely eaten. The buds of the common birch (*Betula alba*) also afford it a portion of its subsistence during the months of winter. In the autumn it eats the berries of the juniper (*Juniperis communis*), the cranberry (*Oxycoccus palustris*), the whortle-berry (*Vaccinium uliginosum*), and numerous other berries which are at that time common in the forests.

The food of the young birds, like that of some of our other game birds, consists in great part of insects of various kinds—ants, worms, &c.

When in captivity they require to be fed with corn; probably any of the cereals, or beans, or peas would be suitable; but they must also be supplied with the twigs of the spruce fir, pine, and juniper, freshly gathered. On such diet as this they have been kept in a healthy condition through the winter in a large loft in Dalecarlia; but during the summer they had more liberty, and bred freely.

As to the food suitable for the young birds reared in this domesticated condition, Mr. Greiff makes the following judicious remarks:—"They are to be supplied with ants' eggs in conjunction with the materials of which the hills of those insects are composed; hard-boiled eggs are to be chopped and mixed amongst fine moistened barley-meal; also pea-haulm and trefoil grass. They must have plenty of water, which must be placed so that they cannot overturn the pitcher, for they suffer very much if they get wet when young.   Dry sand and mould they should never be without. When they get larger, and cabbage-leaves, strawberries, and cranberries, and blue-berries are to be had, they are fond of such food; and when they are full grown, they eat barley and wheat; and in winter they should get young shoots of pine and birch buds.   I have seen many people who thought they treated young birds well by giving them juniper berries; but they never resort to this kind of food but in case of necessity."

The usual method of shooting the Capercaillie by the Scandinavian sportsman is the following :—Mr. Lloyd says, "At this period of the year of which I am now speaking (the autumn), I usually shot the Capercaillie in company with my Lapland dog, Brunette.   She commonly flushed them from the ground; where, for the purpose of feeding upon berries, &c., they are much during the autumnal months.   In this case, if they only saw the dog, their flight in general was short, and they soon perched in the trees. Here, as Brunette had the eye of an Eagle, and the foot of an Antelope, she was not long in following them.   Sometimes, however, these birds were in the pines in the first instance; but as my dog was possessed of an extraordinary fine sense of smelling, she would often wind, or in other words scent, them from a very long distance.   When she found the Capercaillie, she would station herself under the tree where it was sitting, and by keeping up an incessant barking, direct my steps towards the spot.   I now advanced with silence and caution; and as it frequently happened that the attention of the bird was much taken up with observing the dog, I was enabled to approach until it was within the range of my rifle, or even of my common gun. In the forest the Capercaillie does not always present an easy mark when he takes wing from the trees; for, dipping down from the pines nearly to the ground, as is frequently the case, they are often almost out of distance before one can properly take aim. No. 1 or 2 shot may answer very well, at short range, to kill the hens; but for the cocks, the sportsman should be provided with much larger.

"The above plan of shooting the Capercaillie is very commonly adopted throughout Scandinavia, and during the autumnal months in particular, is occasionally attended with considerable success. But I do not speak from much experience, as at that period of the year my time has in general been otherwise occupied. I have, however, killed five of these birds in a single day."

Mr. Lloyd had never used pointers when searching for Capercaillie, but thinks that if steady, and well under command, they would answer very well early in the season; but he inclines to give the preference to such a dog as his Brunette. Mr. Greiff says, "They (the dogs) ought to be rather small; not to bark violently, but only now and then; to hunt only at a short distance from the sportsman; to have a good and sure scent, and to be easily called in. When the frosty nights commence, the Capercaillie sits better to the cocker than at other times."

The nest of the Capercaillie hen is placed upon the ground in some quiet and secluded situation. She lays from six to twelve eggs, on which she sits for twenty-nine days. The young birds run as soon as they are hatched; they remain with the mother till towards the winter, but the cocks leave her sooner than the hens.

The eggs "are two inches three lines long, by one inch eight lines in breadth, of a pale reddish yellow brown, spotted all over with two shades of darker orange brown."

Like other birds, the Capercaillie is found to vary in its plumage. Mr. Lloyd mentions a hen which, with the exception of a few grey feathers, was entirely white. He also states that "The hen Capercaillie occasionally breeds with the cock of the Black Game; the produce of which are in Sweden called 'Racklehanen' (the *Tetrao medius* of authors); these partake of the leading characteristics of both species. Out of twenty 'Racklehanar,' which is the male, no two, according to Mr. Falk, are alike; and the difference of colour, observable among the 'Racklehönan,' which is the female, is still greater. 'Racklehanen' are very seldom to be met with. During my stay in Wermeland, however, Mr. Falk had two of these birds in his possession, and I myself shot a third."

The Capercaillie, in its native forests in the north of Europe, is undoubtedly polygamous, and in any attempt to preserve, it is absolutely necessary to keep down the males, so as not to allow them to approach to anything like an equality in numbers with the females.

In the adult male the bill, which is large, strong, and hooked, is of the colour of horn. The nostrils are small, and nearly concealed under some short feathers, which extend under the throat, and are much longer there than the rest, and are of a black colour. Irides, hazel; over each eye there is a patch of naked skin, of a bright scarlet colour. The feathers of the head and neck are beautifully speckled with greyish white on a brownish black ground; those on the head and throat, rather elongated. The back and upper tail coverts, marked like the head and neck, but not so regularly. Breast, black, richly glossed with dark green at the upper part, and with a few white feathers on the body and thighs. Wings, dark brown, mottled with light brown; wing coverts, the same; under wing coverts, white, showing on the shoulder like a white patch. Sides and flank have the feathers of brownish grey, speckled with black. Tail feathers, eighteen in number, are black, the outside ones with a few white spots. Legs, very strong, covered with brownish grey feathers. Toes and claws black.

The adult female has the bill dark horn, paler at tip. Irides, as in the male. Head and all the upper parts are ochre brown, barred with black or dark brown. Front of neck and breast are brownish orange. The breast feathers, narrowly edged with grey, inside which is a slight band of black. Legs, covered with greyish brown feathers. Toes and claws, pale brown.

The young birds of both sexes resemble the female till the first moult, and the males take three years to acquire the full adult plumage.

The weight of the adult male, Mr. Lloyd says, varies much in different localities; thus in Lapland they seldom exceed nine or ten pounds; in Wermeland they will reach thirteen pounds; while in the southern provinces of Sweden they will reach seventeen pounds and upwards. The hen Capercaillie seldom much exceeds five or six pounds.

In Scotland Mr. Harvie-Brown states that the weight of the male rarely exceeds ten pounds, and that of the female four and a half.

In length the adult male Capercaillie varies considerably; but its usual length is from two feet nine to three feet four inches. The females vary from one foot ten to two feet two or three inches in length.

We have various accounts as to the desirableness of the Capercaillie as an article of food. By some they are pronounced to be coarse and ill-flavoured; by others they are considered, particularly the females, to be excellent. Mr. Greiff, a Swedish gentleman of high rank as a sportsman, says, as quoted by Mr. Lloyd, "of the supply this bird furnishes to the larder, and the delicious dish it forms when brought to table, every one knows the value." We have on several occasions partaken of this bird at table, and although we should not say it was coarse or disagreeable, still it certainly possessed somewhat the turpentiney flavour one might expect it to have when feeding on the pine leaves.

This discrepancy in the accounts of the Cock of the Woods, as a bird for the table, may, we think, probably be very readily explained. The times when we have had opportunities of tasting this bird were on each occasion rather late in the winter, when they had, for a considerable period, been feeding on the pine leaves chiefly; we can easily conceive this bird in autumn, when feeding on the various wild berries, then so prevalent, to be very superior in flavour to one which for several months had subsisted almost wholly on the turpentiney leaves of the pine.

Lord Lilford, writing of the Capercaillie, states that "The flesh of the young birds is, in my opinion, superior to that of black game, and I have found that even the old cocks may, by judicious culinary treatment, be rendered into very palatable food."

BIBLIOGRAPHY.

Lloyd's "Game Birds and Wild Fowl of Sweden and Norway" contains a very full description of the history of this species as it exists in the north of Europe.

Yarrell's "British Birds," 4th edition, by H. Saunders, has a very complete account of this species.

Dresser's "Birds of Europe," Vol. VII., gives a full scientific description, with coloured illustrations, of the species and its hybrids.

Harvie-Brown's "Capercaillie in Scotland" furnishes an admirable account of the reintroduction of the species into Great Britain.

THE BLACK GROUSE

BLACK COCK—GREY HEN.

Tetrao tetrix, ... LINNÆUS.

Tetrao, a bird mentioned by Pliny.
Tetrix, a bird mentioned by Aristotle.

Tétras lyre, French; *Biskhahn ♂*, German; *Berkhoen*, Dutch; *Cua furuda*, Spanish; *Aarhane*, Danish; *Orre*, Swedish; *Aarfugl*, Norwegian; *Tetereff, Kosach, Poliasch ♀, Riadbushka*, Russian.

THE Black Grouse, being a native of Great Britain, is very generally distributed wherever situations agreeable to its habits are found. In the south of England it occurs in the New Forest, in Hampshire; in Devonshire, near Axmouth, and on the wild country of Dartmoor, Sedgemoor, and Exmoor, as well as on Lord Caernarvon's estates near Dulvarton; in Sussex, on Ashdown Forest; in Surrey in several localities. In Somerset they are no longer abundant, but occur on the higher ground near Taunton, and elsewhere; and in Worcestershire, Staffordshire, Derbyshire, Lancashire, Yorkshire, Cumberland, and Northumberland; becoming more plentiful as we proceed north, till in Scotland they become abundant. It is plentiful in Sutherland wherever it has any protection; and according to Macgillivray, is found in the Isles of Mull and Skye, but not in Orkney or Shetland. A few are met with in Wales. In Ireland it does not exist; and from what Mr. W. Thompson states, it is very doubtful whether any have ever existed there beyond those brought over and turned out with the hope that they would breed. This hope, however, does not appear to have been ever realised; some natural or local cause seems to have interfered in each instance, although every care and protection was offered the birds.

The following accounts of this attempted introduction into Ireland are interesting, and we give them in the hope of directing particular attention to the providing the young in any future experiments with the food which they seem to require, and which in these instances was wanting. We take them both from Mr. Thompson's " Natural History of Ireland." The first is a letter to Mr. Thompson from C. Redmond, gamekeeper to Viscount O'Neil, at Claggan, dated January 1, 1841 :—" Twelve years ago (two years previous to my coming here), there were four brace of Black Game turned out, a cock and hen of which I frequently met with outside the plantations in the heath, my dogs setting them like Grouse. They were never to be seen together, but kept a mile separate, and each of them always about the same place. The hen I found dead three years ago, and supposed her to have been shot at by a party which Lord O'Neil had there at that time; the cock has left us, or been killed also. I saw a cock that was shot last year at Glenariff, near Cushendall (some miles distant), which may have been the same. I was at the letting out of nine Black Game in 1832 in this place, and a single bird I never saw afterwards. The reason I cannot assign; it might be that they wandered away, which I believe they are prone to do, or were hurt in coming from Scotland, and died."

The next account is from John Inglis, gamekeeper to Mr. Edmund McDonnell, at Glenarm Park, also in January 1841. He says:—" In reply to your note regarding Black Game, I am sorry I cannot give a very flattering account of them. There has been one Black Cock here about four years; I have not seen him for the last four or five weeks, but I suppose him to be still alive. I think it is likely he came from Claggan, as I believe Lord O'Neil turned out some there shortly before the bird was seen here. (The places are about fifteen miles apart.) At the beginning of August 1839, I went to Scotland, and got nine young birds at Douglas Castle. Two of them died on the passage. I turned out the remaining seven on the hill near the place where the old cock used to haunt; but none of them that I know of were ever seen afterwards. The reason I assign for their not succeeding at this time is, that they were too young, and not fit to manage for themselves without the help of the old bird. In November 1839 I again went to Douglas Castle, got six brace of full-grown birds, namely, seven hens and five cocks; I got them all safe over to Glenarm, where I kept them for two days, feeding them on corn till they recovered from the effects of the passage. I turned them out in the park quite strong and healthy to all appearance. Some time after, one of the cocks was found dead in the park; he was quite light, and thin of flesh. Another of the cocks was shot about the same time in Glenariff, about eight miles from Glenarm. A few of them kept about the park all winter. Sometimes one would be seen, sometimes two, and in the month of March there were three hens and one cock seen together; but about the beginning of May all the hens disappeared, and none of them have been seen since. One cock kept the park all summer, and was seen lately, which is all that I know of here out of the twelve brought over. A cock was shot about two months ago by a gentleman near Ballycastle (about twenty miles distant), which is likely to be another of them. Where all the hens have gone I cannot say; I am in hopes that some of them may be alive yet, as they are so much like Grouse that people who are unacquainted with them would take no notice of them." He then says :—

" I now come to your last query, which is, if they ever bred? and if they did not succeed, the reasons assigned for their not doing so? I really confess that I cannot assign any satisfactory reason whatever, as I have no doubt that full-grown birds would live as well in Ireland as they do in Scotland, if they were only let alone. What I am most doubtful about is, whether they will breed as well; and the reason I am doubtful about this is, that when I was in Scotland, keeper with Lord Douglas, at Douglas Castle, where Black

Game are very plentiful, I used, in hunting the dogs over the ground, to find all the young broods of Black Game, not among heath or moss ground, where young Grouse generally are, but on white or green ground, where sprit or rushes are plentiful, and where you will seldom find young Grouse. But when they get strong and able to do for themselves, they get into packs, often to the number of forty or fifty, and fly over the whole country, and take both to the woods and corn-fields. When at Douglas last, I was talking to Lord Douglas' keeper, about what he thought the young birds fed on. He said that early in the season he had caught some young birds, intending to take them and learn them to feed, so that I might be better able to get them safe over; but they all died in a day or two. He cut open some of their crops to see what they fed on, and could observe nothing but the seed of the sprit or rush. Now, from the number of black cattle that are kept on the mountains in the north of Ireland, there is scarcely any sprit or rushes allowed to grow that would be of any use either for cover or food. I have seldom seen Black Game sit when cattle go near them, and a crow flying over will make a score of them rise and fly away in the latter end of the season, when they are strong on the wing. With respect to the haunts and breeding-ground of young Black Game, I speak only from my own observations. I am not aware that they haunt the same kind of ground in other parts of the country; I merely wish to direct your attention to it. I know there are plenty in the Island of Arran, but do not know what sort of ground they frequent there. As I mentioned before, none of the hens have been seen since the beginning of the breeding time; whether they began to hatch, and were killed by some vermin, or wandered away in search of a more suitable place for their purpose, is a question I cannot answer. Lord Courtown's keeper was at Douglas Castle shortly after I was, in November 1839, and got away six brace to his Lordship's estates south of Dublin; but I have not heard how they succeeded."

A similar want of success has been attendant on birds brought from Scotland, and turned out at Tollemore Park, county of Down. In April 1846 there was still a fine Grey Hen there, but no male bird.

The great difference which usually exists between the food of the young and adult birds of almost all species will readily account for the fact here stated—as to adult birds thriving and doing well, while no broods appear to have been produced; and we can easily imagine the absence of the sprits or rushes in the localities referred to, to have had considerable influence in the above-related negative results as to the Black Game breeding in Ireland. It would be well if those who have the opportunity of doing so, were to examine carefully the crops of young Black Game in all stages of their growth; and if this were well 'and carefully done, and properly recorded, there can be little doubt that we should either soon see the Black Cock introduced into Ireland, or the fact of the impossibility of adding such a desirable bird to the Irish Game List would be proved by the existence of some natural and insuperable bar. We can scarcely think that the somewhat peculiar climate of Ireland offers any absolute impediment to the increase of the Black Grouse; were this the case, we should hardly find it regularly breeding, as we do, in several of the mildest parts of England, such as the extreme south of Devon, where the climate assimilates, in many respects, to that of the Green Isle.

Mr. Thompson hints that Great Britain may be the extreme western range of this fine bird. Even if this were so naturally, we see no reason why the attempts to introduce it artificially should necessarily be unsuccessful; at any rate, until the experiment has been fully tried, by turning out the birds in districts where the natural productions are similar, botanically, to those of the locality from which the birds are brought, the question can hardly be said to be settled. As a matter of choice we should prefer introducing into an open country, birds from a similar situation, in preference to those that had been reared where wood was plentiful.

Over the Continent the Black Grouse is very generally distributed.   In the north of Europe it is found plentifully in Norway, Sweden, Denmark, Russia, and Siberia.   It also occurs in more or less abundance in Lapland, Holland, Poland, Germany, France, Italy, and all through the timbered parts of the Alps.

The habits of the Black Grouse, being less arboreal than those of the Capercaillie, lead it to select such parts of wild and subalpine country as are naturally covered with a thick brushwood of alder, birch, hazel, and willow, along with the rank and luxuriant herbage, such as fern, reeds, rushes, and coarse grass, which is commonly found in such situations.   Such districts as the above are generally well supplied with marshy and boggy ground, which appears to have special attractions for the Black Grouse.   If to these we add wild and sequestered woody glens, not uncommon in such untamed districts, we shall be able to form a correct idea of the usual resorts of this fine bird.   In some favourable localities, however, where considerable quantities of timber exist, the Black Cocks will often frequent them from August until the spring; and in these situations they are said always to roost on the ground, and not in the trees, though they perch readily, and live much on the young shoots of the trees.

In the very severe winter weather of the north of Europe, the Black Grouse, having fed plentifully on the food then attainable, such as the catkins of the birch, buries itself, more or less completely, like the Capercaillie, in the snow; and by thus economising its natural heat, it is able to survive a cold that could not but prove fatal to it if exposed for any time to its full severity.   It is probable that this expedient is much more frequently resorted to than is commonly supposed, by all birds whose habits lead them into such frozen localities.

The males associate together during the autumn and winter months in considerable flocks or packs, and do not separate until the early spring—in March or April.   Being polygamous, these packs now break up, and each male bird chooses some particular station, such as an elevated open piece of ground, from which he endeavours to banish all others of his own sex. Having, by repeated battles, obtained the lordship of his territory, he commences at early day-break or evening twilight to invite the attendance of the females. On these occasions he struts about in a pompous manner, trailing his wings, elevating and expanding his tail, which he occasionally bends to one side, inflating his neck, and in fact proceeding much in the way the Turkey Cock does under similar circumstances. During this proceeding he continues uttering his love-call, which is a peculiar humming, crowing, rolling note, accompanied by a sound, compared by Mr. Selby to the noise made in whetting a scythe. He is at this time in his most brilliant plumage, and the naked wattle over his eye assumes a brighter scarlet. In some well-preserved districts numerous cock birds may be heard at the same time uttering their love-song. On hearing it the females soon assemble on the appointed spot.

The following account of the habits of the Black Grouse in the breeding-season is from the pen of Mr. Archibald Hepburn, a most careful and accurate observer, and is particularly interesting, from its recording a deviation from the ordinary conduct of the cock birds as detailed by other observers :—Mr. Hepburn says, "On the 12th of April 1843, when riding over the green hills which divide the head waters of the Teviot from those of the tributaries of the Esk, I rested for two hours at the inn of Mosspaul ; there, on a sloping hill, I noticed a pack of Black Grouse, consisting of three males and eleven females, feeding within one hundred and fifty yards of the inn door, and fifty yards from the highway on which I stood. One of the former lowered his head, depressed the tips of his wings, erected and expanded his tail, now and then bending it on one side like a Turkey Cock, and strutting about in pompous style before the females, uttered a loud, rumbling, guttural, and at first generally querulous, and then rolling note ; which in that quiet narrow glen was easily heard at the distance of a quarter of a mile. It would be difficult to syllable such a note; the snarling of a mastiff, omitting the nasal part of the performance, gives a pretty correct idea of the rolling notes. The proud bird was a haughty wooer, for aye as each female fled from his importunities, after pursuing her a short way, he paid his addresses to another. It is a curious fact that, although the amorous chase often brought him into close contact with the other two males, who remained silent and unconcerned spectators of his fooleries, 'not the slightest animosity was manifested by either party.' A stage-coach dispersed the pack; two males and eight females flew across the glen; on alighting, one of the former recommenced his gestures and notes, and occasionally uttered a loud, harsh, hissing squeal or scream. By reason of his importunities, as well as to obtain food, the pack soon became scattered; so he was obliged at times to fly from group to group of coy females, scarcely ever intermitting his curious cry when on the ground. A man at the inn informed me that these notes and gestures usually commenced about the middle of March, and ceased in the course of eight or ten weeks. I observed their habits most attentively during the space of an hour and a half, noting down everything of interest; and although this account may differ from that given by other observers, it is too brief, and stands too much alone, to justify any one in contradicting their statements." It is difficult to reconcile the conduct of the two passive males on this occasion with their usually pugnacious disposition, as recorded by numerous other trustworthy observers; may it be that they were two young birds which had been well beaten and conquered by the other, probably an old and powerful bird? We have frequently, in the poultry-yard, seen a similar exhibition of subjection by young cocks, in the presence of the lord of the dunghill.

From the time the females have deposited their proper number of eggs, which is usually in the month of May, and have commenced sitting, they are deserted by the cock birds, who again assemble in small parties, and seek the secluded and quiet thicks, among which they chiefly remain till they have completed their moult. They are, during this seclusion, particularly timid and shy. The female has thus the whole charge of hatching and bringing up the young birds. In their first plumage both sexes resemble the female, and they continue with her until the autumnal moult, when the young males join the old cocks, with whom they then remain till the following spring. The young cocks do not, however, all of them at once obtain their full adult plumage, but for some months some will retain a portion of their younger dress. The packs of male birds are sometimes very numerous, often amounting to from fifty to seventy birds. The females also in autumn are occasionally found in packs, but in much smaller numbers, generally under twenty.

Mr. Daniel, in his "Rural Sports," gives the following description of the methods of shooting and capturing the Black Game in Russia and Siberia. He says, "In Russia the shooting of the Black Grouse is conducted in the following way :—Huts full of loop-holes, like little forts, are built for this purpose in the woods frequented by these birds. Upon the trees within shot of these huts are placed artificial decoy-birds, commonly made of black cloth, with the marks of the natural fowl. As the Grouse assemble, the company fire through the openings, and so long as the sportsman is concealed, the report of the gun does not frighten away the birds ; several of them may therefore be killed from the same tree. If by chance three or four are placed on branches one above the other, the sportsman has only to shoot the undermost bird first, and the others gradually upwards in succession ; the uppermost bird is earnestly employed in looking down after his fellow-companion, and keeps chattering to it till he becomes the next victim.

"During winter in Siberia, they take these birds in the following manner :—A certain number of poles are laid horizontally on forked sticks, in the open forests of birch ; small bundles of corn, by way of allurement, are tied on them, and at a small distance certain tall baskets, of a conic shape, are set, with the broadest part uppermost; just within the mouth of the basket is placed a small wheel, through which passes an axis, so nicely fixed as to admit it to play very readily, and on the least touch, either on one side or the other, to drop down, and again recover its situation. The Black Grouse are soon attracted by the corn on the horizontal poles, first alight upon them, and after a short repast, fly to the baskets, and attempt to settle on their tops, when the wheel drops sideways, and they fall headlong into the trap, which is sometimes found half full."

As might be expected from the nature of the localities chosen by the Black Grouse, the food on which it subsists is subject to considerable variety: thus in the summer it chiefly consists of the flowers of various plants, such as the autumnal hawk-bit (*Apargia autumnalis*), of which it is said to be extremely fond; several species of *Ranunculus*, or buttercup; the various species of chickweed (*Cerastium*); the very numerous tribe of *Carices*, or sedges; common eye-bright (*Euphrasia officinalis*); various grasses; the leaves of some of the small willows; green corn occasionally; and towards the autumn the seeds of various plants; the berries of such alpine plants as the cranberry (*Vaccinium oxycoccos*); the whortleberry (*V. myrtillus*); the cowberry (*V. vitis idæa*); the crowberry (*Empetrum nigrum*); the red bearberry (*Arbutus uva ursi*); together with numerous insects. In the autumn all the berries just named, together with the dried flower heads of the scabious (*Scabiosa succisa*); some of the *Compositæ*, the seeds of the various grasses, oats, leaves of the scabious, the greater plantain (*Plantago major*), the flowers of various *Ranunculi*, the twigs of the ling (*Calluna vulgaris*) and of the cranberry, &c. In the winter months the 'bill of fare' is more circumscribed, consisting chiefly of the twigs of ling, tops of herbaceous plants, young shoots of fir, catkins of birch and hazel, which, as well as the leaves of the ferns, communicate a peculiar flavour to the flesh, leaves of turnip and rape, and what stray grain it can pick up on the stubbles.

Mr. Daniel mentions a curious circumstance in the economy of this bird, that is not endorsed by later writers, which is, that cherries and peas prove fatal to it. He merely mentions it as a fact, and does not say whether it is only an occasional and casual result, or invariably the case.

In sporting language you are said to 'spring' or 'raise' Grouse; you find a 'brood' of Grouse; you kill a 'brace' or a 'leash' of Black Game; and when a number congregate together they are said to 'pack.'

The time fixed by law for shooting Black Game is, in England from the 1st of September to the 1st of December; and in Scotland from the 20th of August to the 10th of December. It is, however, very generally thought by sports-men that it would be a great advantage in every way if a later date were fixed both for commencing this shooting, and also for its termination. It is probable that if the time for shooting Black Game were made the same as for shooting Pheasants, the change would be very advantageous; for the birds would have sufficient time to arrive at tolerable maturity, and the sportsman would have much greater satisfaction in bagging such birds than the wretched 'pouts,' which it is always a matter of regret to the true sportsman to see shot.

It is a somewhat curious circumstance that the Black Grouse alone of all our Game Birds, not even excepting the noble Capercaillie, should have been selected as worthy of the honour of being considered ROYAL GAME; and whenever warrants are issued to kill game in the New Forest, the Black Cock is always excepted, along with the Red and Fallow Deer.

It was at one time thought that where the Black Grouse increased the Red Grouse diminished, but it is now very generally considered that this effect does not take place, and indeed the habits of the birds are sufficiently different to render such a supposition improbable; thus we find the Black Grouse frequenting moist situations and woody covers, while the Red Grouse inhabits the more elevated and dry moors covered alone with heather; their breeding-places, too, are equally distinct in character. At the commencement of the shooting season the Black Cock will lie like a stone, but later on he becomes very wild, and extremely difficult to approach.

The situation chosen by the female Black Grouse for her nest is usually in some rough marshy place, well covered with long coarse grass and herbage; on the ground, under one of these tufts or some low bushy shrub, she places her nest, which is of the most simple construction, being composed of a few dried stems of grass. In this she deposits her eggs, varying in number from six to ten. They are in colour yellowish white, speckled and blotched with reddish brown, and measure two inches in length, by one inch and five lines in breadth. Soon after the young birds are produced, they are taken by the mother to more elevated regions, where, however, a rank and coarse herbage will generally be found, along with boggy moist ground, and but little heather.

According to the author of "The Moor and the Loch," the principal food of the young birds consists of the brown seeds of a short thick rush, near which the hen and young may always be found, and which is easily seen on the moor. This fact, as we have before hinted, should be borne in mind in any future attempts to introduce the Black Grouse into the sister country.

Various efforts have at different times been made to domesticate the Black Grouse, but as yet without success, although they have bred while in a state of captivity; and not only live, but individually do well in confinement.

As in other gallinaceous birds, barren female Black Grouse will assume more or less completely the plumage of the male; the change, however, is usually limited to the presence of some black feathers among their ordinary plumage.

Sir William Jardine possessed "a female, or Grey Hen, shot by the late Sir Sidney Beckwith, entirely of a dull whitish grey, having the cross markings of a darker and browner shade." The rarity, however, of records of varieties of the Black Grouse prove that these changes are by no means common; and it is a well-known fact that certain species of birds are seldom, if ever, found to vary from the normal standard, while others are subject to constant variations. Domestication has doubtless a great influence in educing variations in colour, and we accordingly find many domesticated birds losing almost entirely the characteristic colour of their wild prototypes; as, for example, the Tame Duck, the Goose, and many breeds of the Barn-door Fowl. The colours, if we may so call them, usually involved in these changes, are black and white and their mixtures, and perhaps, but more rarely, brown.

Like the Pheasant and the Capercaillie, the Black Grouse will now and then breed with other closely allied birds; numerous hybrids between this bird and the Pheasant, varying a good deal, probably as the union was between a Black Cock and a hen Pheasant, or between a cock Pheasant and a Grey Hen, are upon record. Of such hybrids Mr. Yarrell has enumerated thirteen examples; but others might probably without much difficulty be added. Birds have also been obtained in Norway which are believed to be hybrids between the Black Grouse and a species of Ptarmigan, but they are stated to be extremely rare; those between it and the Capercaillie have already been described. It has also been known in Sweden to breed with the Barn-door Fowl, and, it is also suspected, with the Red Grouse.

The male Black Cock has the bill dusky black; irides, dark blue; over each eye is a semi-lunar patch of naked bright scarlet skin; under each eye there is a spot of dirty white colour. Head, neck, breast, back, and rump, all of a rich black, reflecting steel blue and purple; quills, brown; secondaries and wing coverts, tipped with white, and forming a white bar across the wing; the bastard wing has also a spot of white on it. Belly, wing coverts, and tail, pitch black; the tail, which consists of sixteen feathers, is deeply forked, the outside feathers curving outwardly; the end of the outside one seems as if cut off; under tail coverts, pure white. Legs and thighs, covered with dark brown, mottled with white feathers; legs, feathered to the toes, which have lateral fringes.

In the female, or Grey Hen, as in the male, the bill is

dusky black, and there is the same dusky white patch beneath the eye.   The head and neck are ochre yellow, rayed with black; the upper parts are brownish orange, as a ground colour, barred and speckled with black; throat, breast, and belly, of a yellowish white or very pale orange, barred with black; the feathers on the wings and shoulders have the centre black, but the shaft is of a pale colour, which gets broader and paler towards the tip; greater wing coverts, tipped with white.   The tail, consisting of eighteen feathers, is very slightly forked, of a reddish brown, spotted with black, the tip greyish white; under tail coverts, white, with a few bars of orange and black.

The young birds resemble the female in plumage until the autumnal moult.

The weight of an adult Black Cock is usually under four pounds, but has been known to reach four and a half pounds; that of the female is from two to two and a half pounds.

The cock bird measures in length from one foot ten inches to two feet, while the female seldom exceeds eighteen inches.

As an article of food the Black Grouse is generally much admired, though certainly by no means equal to the Red Grouse. It is remarkable in having the greater and lesser pectoral muscles of different colours—the outside or greater one being very dark; while the lesser one, nearest the breast bone, is remarkably white, and is the favourite part with the epicure.

BIBLIOGRAPHY.

Lloyd's "Game Birds and Wild Fowl of Sweden and Norway," contains a full description of the habits of the species in the north of Europe.

Dresser's "Birds of Europe," Vol. VII., gives the fullest information as to the distribution, habits, &c., of this species, with coloured illustrations.

Yarrell's "British Birds," 4th edition, by Howard Saunders, may be referred to for further particulars respecting this species.

THE RED GROUSE

RED GAME—MOOR COCK—GOR COCK.

Lagopus scoticus, ... LATHAM.

Lagopus. Lagos—A hare. *Pous*—A foot.
Scoticus—Of or belonging to Scotland.

Red Grouse, Moor-fowl, Muir-fowl, Muir-cock, Gor-cock, Red Ptarmigan,
English ; *Coileachfruoch, Cearc-fhraoich,* Gaelic.

WE are not, we believe, singular in regretting that this bird, an exclusive inhabitant of the British Isles, including, of course, Ireland, does not bear the title of *Britannicus* instead of *Scoticus* ; the former would accurately describe its habitat, while the latter clearly perpetuates error ; for although Scotland certainly possesses it, so also do England, Wales, and Ireland, and each might with equal propriety claim the honour of having its name attached to this admirable and universally esteemed Game Bird. *Scoticus,* however, appears to have been the original specific name, and therefore, according to the rule now adopted regarding scientific nomenclature, must be that by which the bird is designated.

The Red Grouse, or, as it may be simply called, *par excellence,* the Grouse, is very generally distributed over many parts of these Islands where suitable heathy districts prevail. It occurs in Staffordshire, Derbyshire, Lancashire, Yorkshire, Durham, Westmoreland, Cumberland, and Northumberland, in more or less plenty, and is abundant in all the wild districts so prevalent among the Highlands of Scotland.

The mountainous districts of South Wales down to Glamorgan are supplied with it, but not in any great abundance.

In Ireland it is generally distributed over the wild tracts of heathy country prevalent in so many parts of the island, although not in the abundance in which it is found in Scotland.

The Moor Cock, as a bird for the table, is greatly superior to any of the other British Grouse, and indeed can hardly, we think, be equalled by any other Game Bird; it is therefore somewhat singular that so delicious a bird should have been omitted at the celebrated feast given by Archbishop Neville; but neither it nor the Black Grouse appear in the list of the dainties which were served up at that sumptuous entertainment.

The situations chosen by the Red Grouse for its usual resorts are those parts of moorland country which are entirely heathy in character, being those, indeed, which are intermediate in situation between the lofty, barren, and stony tracts frequented by the Ptarmigan, and the lower, swampy, and more wooded districts which we have described as the haunts of the Black Grouse. A supply of heath upon dry ground, however, appears to be the only absolute necessity, elevation above the sea-level not seeming to have much influence on their presence, as we find them in many districts in situations but slightly raised above the sea-shore. Mr. Thompson records that his "friend Mr. John Sinclaire, of Belfast, who has been a regular Grouse-shooter for upwards of sixty years, has not only found Grouse occasionally in stubble and grass fields a mile distant from the mountain heath about Ballantrae, Ayrshire, but has sprung them from the heath growing in plantations of young trees about fifteen feet in height." This would seem to bear out the remark made by Sir W. Jardine that "the habits of the birds have considerably changed. By the approaches of cultivation to the higher districts, and by insulated patches of grain even in the middle of the wildest, the Grouse have learned to depend on the labours of the husbandman for their winter's food, and instead of seeking a more precarious subsistence, during the snow, of tender heath-tops or other mountain plants, they migrate to the lower grounds and enclosures, and before the grain is removed, find a plentiful harvest. Hundreds crowd the stooks in the upland corn-fields, where the weather is uncertain, and the grain remains out even till 'December's snows;' while in the lower countries they seek what has been left on the stubble or ploughed fields."

The Red Grouse is not naturally a wild bird, and in places where they were but little molested, they have allowed us to approach within a short distance of them without appearing frightened; if, however, they are much disturbed, they become extremely wary and shy, and require the utmost care and skill to circumvent them. The colour of the birds assimilating so closely to that of the heath among which they live, it is an easy matter to walk over a bird, if it is inclined to lie, as it frequently will, like a stone.

But although heath-clad hills are the usual and ordinary haunts of the Red Grouse, one or two have occasionally been met with in localities widely different in every respect. Mr. Archibald Hepburn thus records one such occurrence:— "Familiar as I have been for many years past with their habits, I should have been the last to imagine that in any instance one of this species would voluntarily leave its native haunts, and take up its residence among drifting sand-hills, overgrown with bent grass (*Agrostis*), such as stretch along our coast from Whitberry Point to Scoughall Burn, about six miles as the Crow flies from the nearest heath-clad slope of the Lammermoors. It was here that a solitary female was seen in the winter of 1841; and in the following summer Mr. Martine, gamekeeper to the Earl of Haddington, found her attended by a brood of young ones, which arrived at maturity, and frequented their native haunts for several months, till the whole were killed by poachers, or otherwise destroyed." Mr. Thompson says that he has twice in twenty years known single Grouse killed on a low and narrow bare strip of land called the Kinnegar, which stretches in a direction parallel to the nearest line of coast, a miniature promontory, into the bay of Belfast, about four miles from the town.

The flight of the Grouse is very rapid, particularly when they fly down wind, as they generally will do, contrary to the custom of most birds; the rapidity of their flight on such occasions is perfectly astonishing, and they have been known to escape from a falcon in full pursuit, by sheer swiftness of wing.

The Red Grouse is strictly monogamous, differing in this respect from the Capercaillie and Black Cock. The time of pairing varies with the mildness or severity of the season; should it prove mild and open, they will be found mated as early as January, and Selby says occasionally "even previous to that time." The female usually commences laying in March and April, and very rarely even in February, for Mr. Daniel says that "on the 5th of March 1794, the game-keeper of Mr. Lister (now Lord Ribblesdale), of Gisborne Park, discovered on the manor of Twitten, near Pendle Hill, a brood of Red Grouse, seemingly about ten days old, and which could fly about as many yards at a time. This was an occurrence never known to have happened before so early in the year."

The note or crow of the Moor Game is well described by the following:—'Go, go, go, go, go back, go back;' and according to Macgillivray, "The Celts, naturally imagining the Moor Cock to speak Gaelic, interpret it as signifying 'co, co, co, co, mo-chlaidh, mo-chlaidh;' that is, 'who, who (goes there?), my sword, my sword.'" Besides this crow, it has an alarm-note which may be represented by the syllable 'kok' several times repeated. This must have been heard by every one who has disturbed Grouse.

The illegal destruction of Grouse has greatly increased of late years since the introduction of sheep and black cattle on hills formerly tenanted only by Grouse and Red Deer; for among the hinds, or people who attend upon these, too many are found able and willing to poach these birds. The following description of the method by which this is generally

effected is from the pen of a 'Veteran Sportsman :'—
"When Grouse are taken by the net, it is principally by
persons who reside on the moors, or on the borders of
them, such as farmers, and a description of persons to be
found in Yorkshire and the north of England who are
called hinds, who attend the sheep and cattle of the larger
farmer, and dwell at some distance on the moors. These
persons, or at least such of them as are inclined to poaching, watch the motions of Grouse towards evening, when
the birds are about to take up their abode for the night;
and they are already aware of the direction in which they
may expect the evening assemblage from indubitable in-
dications left by the birds on similar previous occasions,
which their constant habit of traversing the ground has
enabled them to notice; and it may be here observed that
Grouse, like Partridges, have their feeding and their sleeping
ground, and if not much molested, will not quit either.
Having watched the birds take up their position for the
night, they prepare the net, and after they have become
still for an hour or two, they approach, and endeavour to
cover them. But netting Grouse is necessarily much more
incomplete than the same operation performed upon Partridges; for although both Partridges and Grouse huddle
themselves together precisely in the same manner on these
occasions, yet the nature of the ground occupied by the
latter renders that effective working of the net, which is
easily accomplished with Partridges, impossible when applied
to Grouse. The situations where these birds are found,
and where, indeed, they can alone exist, are covered with
heath, for the most part, which prevents the close contact
of the net with the ground, and therefore some of the brood
generally escape. The net is dropped (not drawn) over the
spot (which has been previously ascertained as nearly as
possible) where the birds are resting; some of them flutter
up against it on feeling or perceiving its approach, become en-
tangled in the meshes, and are taken; others make their escape
by running amongst the heath till they are out of reach."

In many parts of the north of England the miners are more determined poachers; but they are much fairer sportsmen than those above mentioned, using, almost invariably, the gun only. The same writer furnishes us with the following account of the proceedings of these people:—"These men commence operations prior to the 12th of August; Grouse killed by them a week before the season, are buried in the earth, and putrefaction is thus procrastinated. I learned the circumstances from one of the fraternity. Some years since, I visited the extensive shooting-ground of Stainmoor, Yorkshire; and as on similar previous occasions, after ranging the moors till the intense heat of the day came on, exposed to the unsheltered action of a meridian sun, I seated myself by the side of a rivulet, for the purpose of paying my respects to the brandy flask, and swallowing a sandwich. I had not been long in this situation when a man, accompanied by a single dog, approached, and took his seat at the distance of a few yards. There was nothing impudent or disrespectful in his manner, though the long, inferior-looking gun which he carried, and his appearance altogether, were sufficiently intelligible to me, having frequently been placed in similar company prior to this period. After the usual interrogatories on such occasions, as I had not been remarkably successful, he offered me game at four shillings a brace, presenting several fine birds for my examination; one amongst the number was an old cock that had, I should suppose, escaped the deadly tube for four or five, or perhaps six, seasons; he was the largest Red Grouse that ever fell under my observation, and his weight could not have been much less than two pounds: an old male bird seldom reaches more than a pound and a half, and not very often that; the female is considerably less.

"The man was, no doubt, an inveterate poacher; and notwithstanding the habitual cunning of his tribe, there was in his manner a great degree of unaffected and unqualified simplicity. Upon remarking to him that his birds appeared to have been killed several days, and consequently before the legal commencement of the shooting-season, he unhesitatingly replied that the fine cock which I then held in my hand he had shot four days prior to the 12th of August. As no kind of game fades so soon as Grouse, and as the weather during this period had been remarkable for heat, I inquired how he had contrived to keep his game so well, as it was still sweet; when he gave me the information related above, and added that the birds he then showed me would keep three days longer. He farther remarked that his fraternity found it requisite to commence their season a week before the gentlemen's season, in order to be prepared with a supply of game for bad shots or unlucky sportsmen, and also for the stage - coaches which crossed Stainmoor on their way from the north to Liverpool, Manchester, and other large towns. It was at a period when percussion guns had not become general; the man, in the most respectful manner, asked me to allow him to look at my double detonators, and when he had satisfied his curiosity, he asked me to give him a little of my gunpowder for the purpose of priming his clumsy-looking flint-lock, his own gunpowder being of that coarse kind used in blasting or blowing up the earth or rock in the process of excavation, and of which the lead-mining poachers no doubt rob their employers. Though coarse gunpowder answered the purpose for the charge in the barrel, yet it was not well calculated, it seems, for the purpose of priming. The sale of Grouse, he observed, had been very bad; he had still a considerable stock on hand; he lowered his price to tempt me to purchase, which I declined; and when at length he took his departure, in return, I suppose, for my generosity in supplying him abundantly with priming powder, he pressed me to accept a brace of his Grouse, which, it is almost unnecessary to remark, I declined."

Large numbers of Grouse are snared in the oat-fields of the cottagers and small farmers who live near the moors. The Grouse are very fond of oats as a variety to their more ordinary fare, and frequent these fields in large numbers; and as the approach of a keeper is always easily seen at a considerable distance in such situations, the poacher has ample time to remove all trace of his nefarious deeds before he comes up.

"Grouse, generally speaking, become wild, and even unapproachable, by the beginning or the middle of October; but as soon as a fall of snow happens to take place, so as to cover the ground, these fellows sally forth with a white shirt, or something of the sort, as their outer garment. The birds on these occasions may be seen at a considerable distance, and the poachers contrive to make their appearance resemble, as much as possible, that complexion which the snow has given to the moor and mountains; and being intimately acquainted with what, in place of a more expressive term, may be called the localities of these lofty regions, they are enabled to approach within gunshot, and thus supply the market, at a period when this description of game very easily obtains an increase of price. Severe weather induces the Grouse to pack; but as soon as a mild interval ensues, the males commence the call of courtship. The female will seldom answer the call for some days, or perhaps a week. Here again the poacher sets to work. Many of these miners can imitate the voice of the female bird to such perfection that the cock instantly answers, takes a short flight towards the place whence the invitation seemed to proceed, and calls again. The poacher, concealed by one of the gullies worn by the mountain torrent, or behind a convenient eminence, repeats the note of the female; the cock continues his approaches till within a dozen yards, when he commences a sort of fantastic manœuvre, flying or flirting up from the ground two or three yards, and down again; he does not continue long at this work ere he receives his quietus—in the act of endeavouring to exhibit himself to the concealed female, as he supposes, the poor bird loses his life."

These poachers are very bold and fearless, and will follow their unlawful pursuit in spite of any force of gamekeepers that may be sent after them. We remember once reading of a large party of them besieging the Duke of Norfolk in one of his seats, and requesting (Quere, ' More regali ') a day's shooting over his moors, and saying that they would afterwards avoid them, and only visit those of other proprietors. The necessary licence having been obtained, they, it is said, faithfully kept to their part of the agreement, and abstained from troubling his moors during the rest of the season. Probably the best method is for the keepers to endeavour to identify any visitors on the moors by means of the telescope, with which every keeper should be supplied, instead of a gun; he might then summon the intruder, without the risk of being shot for executing the duties of his office.

In addition to the poachers, the Grouse suffer much from their eggs and young becoming the prey of various rapacious birds, among which, as most destructive, the Carrion Crow (*Corvus corone*) stands pre-eminent. The Eagle, Peregrine Falcon, Hen Harrier, and Buzzard all commit great depredations on the Moor Game; and they are also preyed upon by wild cats, foxes, and the larger *Mustelinæ*. Many eggs are also destroyed by the dogs of those tending sheep, &c., on the moors; and whole broods are also very frequently annihilated by the very destructive system of burning the moors, to render them more suitable pasture-grounds, and which is prevalent in many districts, particularly in Ireland. This burning is used chiefly where sheep are pastured, and is frequently performed in spring, when the birds are sitting; but even if carried on in the autumn, the Grouse would lose both food and shelter, and their numbers must therefore be greatly diminished by this practice.

We come now to consider the food of the Red Grouse; this, from the nature of their haunts, is not of a very varied character, though it is probable that a careful examination of their crops might materially extend the following list:—The whortleberry (*Vaccinium myrtillus*), the cranberry (*V. oxycoccos*), the cowberry (*V. vitis idæa*), the hare-tail cottongrass (*Eriophorum vaginatum*), the smooth heath bedstraw

(*Galium saxatile*), various grasses, sedges or *Carices*, willows, the heath (*Erica cinerea*), the ling (*Calluna vulgaris*), the crowberry (*Empetrum nigrum*), the red bearberry (*Arbutus uva ursi*), oats in their season, &c. During the autumn the fruits of all these plants are eaten, while during the winter months they are obliged to be contented with their tender tops and small branches. As before mentioned, during this season they derive much of their food in some districts from the stubbles and oat-fields. Mr. Thompson mentions that the mountains about Aberarder, which are covered with the reindeer lichen (*Cladonia rangiferina*), with only a sprinkling of heath, were well supplied with Grouse.

The sporting terms applied to the Red Grouse are the same as those given to the Black Game.

Grouse-shooting commences, as is well known, on the 12th of August in England and Scotland.

It is to be regretted that so early a day should have been fixed for this shooting; and were the moors always closed till September 1st, the sport would be far superior, and the birds more fit for the table. It is well known, too, that early in the season, particularly if the weather be very hot, as it often is, the parent birds are the first to rise, and the old hen is very frequently killed, the young birds lying like stones; a known breeding bird is thus destroyed, and the chances for next season, *pro tanto*, diminished. Of course a vast number of poults or young birds are also shot, very often when they can scarcely top the heather; there is no sport in this, and we can hardly imagine a true sportsman bagging such game; being shot too generally at very short distances, they are often almost blown to rags. All these evils would be remedied were the moors kept closed till the 1st of September; in late seasons this delay is doubly necessary.

The following remarks on Grouse-shooting, by Mr. St. John, are penned from a feeling which it would be well were it more frequently exhibited by sportsmen, who, if they do not combine an admiration of the beauties of nature with their love of sporting, lose more than half the true enjoyment of a day on the moors :—" Although, like others, I am excessively fond of this sport, yet I care little for numbers slain ; and when following it independently and alone, am not occupied solely by the anxiety of bagging so many brace. My usual plan when I set out is to fix on some burn, some cool and grassy spring, or some hill summit which commands a fine view, as the extremity of my day's excursion. To this point then I walk, killing what birds come in my way, and after resting myself and dogs, I return by some other route. Undoubtedly the way to kill the greatest number of Grouse is to hunt one certain tract of ground closely and determinedly, searching every spot, as if you were looking for a lost needle, and not leaving a yard of heather untried. This is the most killing system, as every practised Grouse-shooter knows ; but to me it is far less attractive than a good stretch across a range of valley and mountain, though attended with fewer shots. I am also far more pleased by seeing a brace of good dogs do their work well, and exhibiting all their fine instinct and skill, than in toiling after twice the number when hunted by a keeper, whose only plan of breaking the poor animals in is to thrash them until they are actually afraid to use half the wonderful intellect which nature has given them."

The nest of the Red Grouse is placed in a slight hollow under some tuft of ling or heath, which affords a little shelter and concealment ; it is composed of a few straws, or withered grass and ling, with now and then a few of its own feathers, and is of the simplest kind. The eggs, which vary in number from eight to twelve, or even fifteen, are nearly covered with spots and blotches of umber brown, upon a yellowish or reddish white ground ; they measure in length one inch and three - quarters, by one inch and a quarter in breadth. The young run as soon as hatched. Incubation is performed by the female alone ; but the cock bird is seldom far off, and when the young are hatched, assists the female in bringing them up. During the autumn and winter they continue together, and do not separate until the pairing season. During the winter it is a frequent occurrence for several broods to join together, and form packs of forty or fifty birds; they are under such circumstances extremely wary and wild, and are with great difficulty obtained by the sportsman.

The Red Grouse is readily domesticated, and becomes very tame and familiar, and they have even bred when in confinement; Daniel mentions several instances of this, and Sir William Jardine says he has known a brood hatched under a kitchen dresser. The following graphic account of the rearing of a tame covey is taken from the *Field*:—

"Now the history of these tame birds is as follows:—A friend of mine—one who delights in all matters relating to the habits of wild birds, and, what is more, is thoroughly versed in the subject—had a nest of Grouse eggs hatched out under a Hen—this on the same ground where his young Pheasants were being reared. When first out of the egg, the young Grouse showed a disposition to stray somewhat too far from the maternal coop; but this little difficulty was easily overcome by the intelligent keeper. At some distance a wire-netting was placed round the coop. In a very short time this was removed; but to show the result of habit and training on birds, it was found that the young ones circled round much about the place where the wire-netting had stood.

"Time went on, and they soon settled into the habits of their Pheasant companions. Some six or seven grew up, and about October the cock birds seem to have made advances to the hens, and their overtures doubtless being taken by the latter as inopportune—out of season—they modestly levanted. There remained three cocks, all in splendid plumage and condition, feeding, be it remembered, entirely on Pheasants' food and what they could pick up about the house. One of the birds remained in the corner of the field where the coop had stood, taking possession of it for himself. Here at all times he was to be seen ready to dispute his ground with any one passing near it. Usually he challenged with a call, and then, if approached, he was ready either for a fight or to be fed, or both—anything that suited the whim of the intruder.   One day, when I was giving some maize to my friend, the keeper came up, and going on all fours, began throwing grass in the face of the bird.   At once the Grouse responded to the challenge by flying at him, coming up sideways, and using his spurs.   The bird allowed itself repeatedly to be caught, and the moment he was liberated returned again and again to the unequal combat.   More than once have I seen this same bird fly across from his corner and join us when shooting on the opposite woodland bank, this being some 600 or 700 yards across a narrow neck of sea at the head of a loch.   My friend's dogs—retrievers and spaniels—knew the bird well, and paid no attention to him, nor did he to the shots that were fired close to him.   But not so my retriever.   He began by thinking it was his manifest duty to bring the bird to me; but on being duly warned, and on seeing the Grouse trying to get to close quarters to ram him, so to speak, with his spurs, a feeling of alarm, droll to see, came over the dog.   Evidently he concluded he had to deal with something quite new to him, possibly a demented Grouse.   Another day I fell in with my friend a mile from this spot, and having two dogs with me, it was as much as I could do to beat a hasty retreat into a thick wood, so anxious was he to have a spurring match with one or other of the dogs.

"This bird has now taken up his quarters close to a house a mile from the place he was reared, remaining just as tame, and coming regularly for his breakfast.   The two others remain about the lodge, in the courtyard, in the garden, and frequently come in at the servants' dinner-time to pick up anything that may be thrown to them.   They have induced one wild bird to come down off the moor, and this bird is now fairly tame—that is to say, he will let one get within a few yards of him.   When, by the way, it pleased Master Grouse to join us out shooting, if by chance a spaniel came suddenly upon him, he was not in the least degree disconcerted

—he would simply fly on to a rock and begin crowing at the dog."

It is well known that Grouse are afflicted more or less extensively, in some seasons to a very disastrous extent, by an epidemic which is so well known that it is called "The Disease." This has been investigated by many medical men and scientists, but its true nature was finally pointed out in a series of investigations undertaken, at the request of the *Field*, by Dr. Klein, who finally incorporated his results in his work on "The Grouse Disease." This work is hardly one that is adapted for the non-professional reader, unless he be deeply interested in the subject and has some knowledge of bacteriology; but the practical results of it are most important. The following account of the disease, abstracted from Dr. Klein's researches, is from the pen of the editor of this edition, Mr. Tegetmeier, who writes as follows:—

"The external signs of the disease—in the loss of feather on the leg, the general emaciation of the bird, and the darker colour of the feathers on the back and wings—are well known. The internal post-mortem appearances may be thus described: redness occurs in patches in the intestines and the peritoneum or serous membrane which covers them, and also lines the internal surface of the walls of the body; the liver is very much congested with blood, and one or generally both lungs are also much more congested than natural. These are signs that may be noted by any intelligent observer. The microbes or bacteria (which can only be observed by skilled microscopic and pathological observers) are present in large quantities, and may be developed and cultivated in the usual manner by adding a drop of blood to the surface of moist gelatine, when they are developed so rapidly as to become innumerable; and the inoculation with the smallest portion of this gelatine disseminates the disease. These microbes will not only grow on gelatine, but will be developed on vegetable substance, such as potato; and as they are voided in the excrement, it is obvious that they may be left on the moor, remain sheltered in the soil, and give rise to a new epidemic in the following season. Dr. Klein, who has made a more scientific examination of this disease than any other pathologist, is of opinion that there are always cases of diseased birds in the country, and that the disease may become epidemic whenever circumstances favour its development, in precisely the same way that cholera, scarlet fever, diphtheria, and typhoid affect the human race. The occurrence of the disease on one moor or a series of moors, whilst others remain free, he regards as precisely identical with the fact that a corresponding irregularity is noticed in epidemics that affect human beings. The birds on one moor may be in a fitter condition to receive the disease than on another; birds affected with the disease may carry it to one locality, but not to the one next to it. These are points which do not affect the question of the Grouse disease being epidemic and infectious. The secondary causes which he thinks tend to the development of the disease are bad seasons, bad food, and overstocking. These conditions are applicable to all infectious disorders. A weakened individual does not resist the infection as readily as a strong one. If there are many weakly birds on an overstocked moor, if one takes the infection, he starts it amongst the others. The Grouse disease itself may be regarded as an infectious fever or acute infectious pneumonia, which in severe cases will carry off birds while they still remain plump and in good condition; in others they may live, although they are reduced to mere skeletons.

"The presence of tapeworm, which was formerly suggested as being the cause of the disease, is now regarded as accidental. Tapeworms, it is true, are very frequently present in diseased birds, but they are also present in others which are not in the slightest degree affected.

"The congestion of the lungs produces the alteration of the natural voice of the bird, which is so frequently noted; and also the condition of the feathers, and the want of their natural metallic lustre. The birds that die in the spring retain much of their plumpness, the crop is often full, and the lungs are not diseased; the disease, being severe, has killed the Grouse rapidly. Whether the animals are examined in the spring or the autumn, the liver is uniformly congested and soft, being either very dark red or almost black.

"The results drawn from Dr. Klein's observations are, that the disease always exists to a greater or less extent in the country, and that it is only in unfavourable seasons, or under unfavourable conditions, as when a diseased bird finds its way to a somewhat overstocked moor, that it breaks out with great intensity. No remedial treatment or preventive measures can be employed ; all that can be done is to adopt the usual sanitary precautions of not overstocking, of seeing that there is abundant food, and of killing down diseased or infected birds."

In tone of colouring the Red Grouse varies considerably ; thus in some districts all the Grouse are dark, while in others they are light coloured. There is strong probability that these are varieties, by which the birds assimilate their colours to those of the ground they frequent. Mr. W. Thompson was of this opinion, and mentions that "a friend who shot over the moor of Glenroy, Invernesshire, in 1844, observed that the Grouse differed much in their plumage, and were of three varieties, each keeping particularly to its own quarters. On the darkest and most heathy ground were the darkest birds, and the largest, weighing generally two pounds, and sometimes two pounds two ounces ; on the rocky parts they were of a very much lighter brown ; while on the stony and heathy ground combined, they were of an intermediate brown, mottled more or less with white."

These differences in tint can hardly be called varieties, in the usual meaning attached to the term ; but those bred upon the moors of Blanchland, in the county of Durham, as mentioned by Mr. Selby, and which are of a cream-colour, or light grey, spotted more or less with dark brown and black, and occur in considerable numbers, are true varieties ; and it is to be regretted that the breed is not allowed to increase more than seems to be the case. Sir W. Jardine possessed "a Grouse, shot on the moors of Galloway, where the ground colour is nearly yellowish white, and all the dark markings are represented by pale reddish brown; the quills are dirty white. In some instances the plumage takes an opposite shade, and is remarkable for its deep tint and the almost entire absence of markings. The whole or a part of the quills are often found white." A cream-coloured Grouse was shot, says Mr. Archibald Jerdon, in Northumberland, in August 1843; the markings were similar to those on the common Grouse; the ground colour being a cream or light brownish white, and the markings of the same colour, but darker; the quills and greater wing coverts were a bluish grey, as was also the abdomen. It was a young bird.

The adult male Red Grouse has the bill black; nostrils covered by small red and black feathers that hide half the bill; irides, hazel; over each eye is a naked semi-lunar patch of bright scarlet skin, fringed at the edge; there is a white spot on each side of the base of the lower mandible. General ground colour of the plumage, rich sienna brown, shading on the belly into a nearly pure black; tips, paler, and with nearly black wavy lines across each feather. Tail, even, of sixteen feathers; the four centre ones with transverse black lines on chestnut brown ground; all the others, black. Legs and feet, thickly covered to the claws with soft white feathers; claws, greyish white, broad, and strong.

The adult female has the general ground colour of a lighter shade, and the pale markings somewhat larger in size.

The young at first resemble the female, but are more ochreous in colour, and the plumage is more barred. Until they attain their full plumage, they often exhibit, to a greater or less extent, some white feathers on the under parts.

In weight the Grouse would appear to be subject to considerable variety; they have been recorded as attaining the weight of two pounds, but this must be of very rare occurrence. Mr. James Blaydon met with one in 1848, near Pont-y-Pool, which weighed thirty ounces; and in the same year Mr. J. B. Fielding, of Alershole, near Todmorden, shot one weighing thirty-one ounces. The common weight, however, of these birds is from twenty to twenty-two ounces, though an addition of an ounce or two is not uncommon. We have seen one shot by Mr. C. Wilkinson, of Myton, Yorkshire, in September 1851, which weighed full twenty-nine ounces.

The length of the male Red Grouse is sixteen inches; the female is somewhat smaller.

The superexcellence of the Red Grouse as a game bird is universally acknowledged. No method of preparing for the table is superior to plain roasting—Soyer confessed that his "art could not improve grouse;" but grouse are also excellent in game pies, in soup, or as a salmi.

BIBLIOGRAPHY.

MACGILLIVRAY'S "British Birds" contains an admirable account of the structure, habits, and manners of this species.

SEEBOHM'S "British Birds" contains a good account of the species as known on the moors around Sheffield.

"The Grouse" in the "Fur and Feather Series" is chiefly devoted to Grouse shooting by the methods of driving in place of shooting over dogs, a mode of sport which is thus described by Mr. Seebohm:—"Of late years the noble sport of Grouse-shooting has degenerated in too many instances into wholesale slaughter. Instead of shooting a few brace for themselves or their friends, as sportsmen used to do in the good old days, too many owners or renters of moors degrade themselves to the level of bird-butchers. Their only object seems to be to obtain as big a bag as possible, for the unsportsman-like object of turning it into money, or the vulgar pleasure of seeing their names at the head of a long figure in the newspapers."

BOOTH'S "Rough Notes on Birds in the British Islands" contains an admirable account of the experience of the author on the moors, with an engraving of the adult male and female.

DRESSER'S "Birds of Europe," in addition to the accurate and scientific description, contains a full account of the species as it exists in Derbyshire, written by Mr. Seebohm.

THE PTARMIGAN

WHITE GROUSE.

Lagopus mutus, ... MONTIN.

Lagopus. Lagos—A hare. *Pous*—A foot. *Mutus*—Dumb, mute.

Lagopède muet, Gélinotte blanche, French; *Lagopo bianco,* Italian; *Alpen-Schneehuhn, Felsen-Schneehuhn,* German; *Fjeldrype,* Norwegian; *Fjällripa,* Swedish; *Küruna,* Finnish.

THE Ptarmigan, like many of our other birds, has gradually, as cultivation has encroached on its native haunts, become more rare, and in some districts has entirely disappeared; such has been its fate in Cumberland and Westmoreland, where Pennant says it once existed; no traces are, however, now to be found of it in England; and the most southern part of Scotland where it is to be met with is the Grampian range of hills. It becomes more and more plentiful as you go north, among the Highlands, and is also found in the Hebrides, and other isles of Scotland. It is found in Islay, and on the Paps of Jura in considerable plenty. In Ireland it does not exist.

The Ptarmigan of both the European and American continents is generally believed to belong to this species, though the American has been separated under the name of *L. rupestris;* but however this may be, the Ptarmigan must always excite a degree of interest, from the curious phenomenon of its changing in winter, in common with the ermine and alpine hare, from the gay dress of summer to the pure tint which affords it security in its bleak and alpine haunts when covered with their snowy mantle. So admirably adapted, indeed, are its two states of plumage to afford it security, that even the keen eye of the Eagle is very often unable to distinguish it among the surrounding objects which in colour it so closely resembles, unless it chance to excite attention by some unwary motion.

Although the colour of the Ptarmigan must be a very great protection to it from birds of prey and other vermin, there is no doubt that it very frequently affords a meal to the Eagle, as well as the Peregrine Falcon, and other birds of prey. Its ranks are also thinned by the fox and some of the *Mustelinæ*, particularly during the breeding season, when the young are unable to save themselves by flight, and consequently fall an easy prey to their enemies.

The habits of the Ptarmigan lead it to prefer the barren and stony parts of the most elevated ground, instead of the heathy moors within its reach, and which are so essential to the existence of the Red Grouse; among these it lives, and as such districts seldom offer much inducement for man to invade them, they are often left almost unmolested. Still in some localities the shepherds, who nearly all have guns, nominally to shoot foxes, &c., commit considerable havoc among them. Some amount of protection should therefore be afforded to these birds, or even in their Highland homes they may, as in the mountains of Cumberland and West-moreland, gradually become more rare, till at length they are extinct — to the regret of all naturalists, if not of sportsmen.

During the winter the Ptarmigans obtain their food by burrowing under the snow; they are thus concealed from observation, and also protected from the inclemency of the weather, which, however severe, but seldom induces them to seek the lower grounds: they are indeed birds of snow. Ptarmigans are by no means so shy and wary as the Red Grouse, but often exhibit such a degree of tameness, almost amounting to stupidity, as to allow themselves to be killed by a stick; when, however, they are much pursued, this tameness disappears, and they become more difficult of approach, though not to the extent exhibited by their congener. When alarmed by any unusual appearance, such as a man, dog, &c., they lie remarkably still, and so similar in colour are they to the ground on which they crouch that it is an easy thing to overlook them entirely, even though they should be only a very few yards distant, unless your attention is particularly called to them by the peculiar cry of the species, which is in such cases uttered by a sentinel on a stone or rock. If you frighten him, he is off immediately, calling to the others, who join him one by one from their crouching concealment.

Their flight, which is rapid, is often of considerable length, frequently not terminating till they reach the opposite hillside. In autumn and winter the Ptarmigans collect in large packs, and, Macgillivray says, even so early as the end of July.

As a sporting bird, there seems to be a very general feeling among sportsmen that it is infinitely inferior to the Red Grouse. Before having any chance of obtaining birds, you must ascend probably to the very top of the highest mountains, and even then you may very easily be disappointed in obtaining the game you seek; and even if you do succeed, your game is very inferior in size and flavour to the Red Grouse, which you might have procured with half the labour. If, however, you seek the Ptarmigan as a naturalist, you are without doubt amply rewarded for your trouble, by adding to your knowledge of the habits and instincts of these birds as exhibited in the wild and rugged places which possess such powerful attractions for them, and which they never voluntarily leave.

Like the Red Grouse, the Ptarmigan is monogamous, and the packs break up early in the spring, when pairing takes place, and the couples distribute themselves in situations suitable for their purpose.

The note of the Ptarmigan is, according to Macgillivray, like the cry of a frog; but it has been compared to the harsh note of the Missel Thrush or Storm Cock.

The food of the Ptarmigan consists of nearly the same substances as that of the Red Grouse, such as the small and tender tops of the various alpine plants before named, berries, and probably insects. The gizzard always contains numerous small stones, which assist it in grinding up the food into a nutritious mass.

During the winter, while the "frost is on the plain," their mountain homes are necessarily exposed to a double portion of cold, and the small streams become frozen into solid ice; on these occasions the Ptarmigans use snow instead of water to quench their thirst; and it is said, so fond are they of snow, that even in summer-time they endeavour to obtain it whenever practicable.

The terms used by sportsmen when speaking of Ptarmigan are the same as those applied to Grouse, and the time of shooting is also the same.

The following account of Ptarmigan-shooting, by Mr. C. St. John, gives a good idea of the pleasures and dangers attending the pursuit of Ptarmigans when snow is on the ground. Accompanied by a shepherd who knew every inch of the ground they were going to try, Mr. St. John before sunrise leaves the hut where he had passed the night:—" The sun was not up as we crossed the river on the stepping-stones which the shepherd had placed for that purpose, but very soon the mountain tops were gilded by its rays, and before long it was shining brightly on our backs as we toiled up the steep hillside. My companion, who knew exactly which was the easiest line to take, led the way; deeply covered with snow as the ground was, I should without his guidance have found it impossible to make my way up to the heights to which we were bound. 'I'm no just liking the look of the day either, Sir,' was his remark, 'but still I think it will hold up till near nicht; we should be in a bonny pass if it came on to drift while we were up yonder.' 'A bonny pass indeed!' was my inward ejaculation. However, depending on his skill in the weather, and not expecting myself that any change would take place till night-fall, although an

ominous-looking cloud concealed the upper part of the mountain, I went on with all confidence.

"Our object was to reach a certain shoulder of the hill, not
far from the summit, from which the snow had drifted when
it first fell, leaving a tolerably-sized tract of bare stones, where
we expected to find the Ptarmigans basking in the bright
winter sun. It was certainly hard work, and we felt little of
the cold as we laboured up the steep hill. Perseverance
meets with its reward; and we did at last reach the desired
spot, and almost immediately found a considerable pack of
Ptarmigans, of which we managed to kill four brace before
they finally took their flight round a distant shoulder of the
hill, where it was impossible to follow them. An Eagle dashed
down at the flock of birds as they were just going out of our
sight; but as we saw him rise upwards again empty-handed,
he must have missed his aim. By this time it was near mid-
day, and the clouds were gathering on the mountain top, and
gradually approaching us. We had taken little note of the
weather during our pursuit of the birds; but it was now forced
on our attention by a keen blast of wind which suddenly swept
along the shoulder of the mountain, here and there lifting up
the dry snow in clouds. 'We must make our way homewards
at once,' said I. 'Deed ay! it will no be a canny night,' was
the shepherd's answer. Just as we were leaving the bare
stones, a brace of Ptarmigans rose, one of which I knocked
down; the bird fell on a part of the snow which sloped downwards towards a nearly perpendicular cliff of great height.
The slope of the snow was not very great, so I ran to secure
the bird, which was fluttering towards the precipice. The
shepherd was some little distance behind me, lighting his
everlasting pipe; but when he saw me in pursuit of the
Ptarmigan, he shouted at me to stop. Not exactly understand-
ing him, I still ran after the bird, when suddenly I found the
snow giving way with me, and sliding *en masse* towards the
precipice. There was no time to hesitate, so, springing back
with a power that only the emergency of the case could have
given me, I struggled upwards again towards my companion.

How I managed to escape I cannot tell; but in less time than it takes to write the words I had retraced my steps several yards, making use of my gun as a stick to keep myself from sliding back again towards the edge of the cliff. The shepherd was too much alarmed to move, but stood for a moment speechless; then recollecting himself, he rushed forward to help me, holding out his long gun for me to take hold of. For my own part, I had no time to be afraid, and in a few moments was on *terra firma*, while a vast mass of snow which I had set in motion rolled like an avalanche over the precipice, carrying with it the unfortunate Ptarmigan.

"I cannot describe my sensations on seeing the danger which I had so narrowly escaped. However, no time was to be lost, and we descended the mountain at a far quicker rate than we had gone up it. The wind rose rapidly, moaning mournfully through the passes of the mountain, and frequently carrying with it dense showers of snow. The thickest of these showers, however, fell above where we were, and the wind still came behind us, though gradually veering round in a manner which plainly showed us that it would be right ahead before we reached home. Every moment brought us lower, and we went merrily on, though with certain anxious glances occasionally to windward. Nor was our alarm unfounded, for just as we turned an angle of the mountain, which brought us within view of the shepherd's house perched on the opposite hillside, with a good hour's walk and the river between us and it, we were met by a blast of wind and a shower of snow, half drifting and half falling from the clouds, which took away our breath, and nearly blew us both backwards, shutting out the view of everything ten yards from our faces.

"We stopped and looked at each other. 'This is gey an' sharp,' said the shepherd; 'but we mustn't lose a moment's time, or we shall be smothered in the drift; so come on, Sir;' and on we went. Bad as it was, we did not stop for its abating, and having fortunately seen the cottage for a moment, we knew that our course for the present lay straight down the mountain. After struggling on for some time, we came to a part of the ground which rather puzzled us, as, instead of being a steep slope, it was perfectly flat; a break, however, in the storm allowed us to see for a moment some of the birch trees on the opposite side of the river, which we judged were not far from our destination. The river itself we could not see, but the glimpse we had caught of the trees guided us for another start, and we went onwards as rapidly as we could, until the storm again closed around us, with such violence that we could scarcely stand upright against it. We began now at times to hear the river, and we made straight for the sound, knowing that it must be crossed before we could reach home, and hoping to recognise some bend or rock in it which would guide us on our way.

"At last we came to the flat valley through which the stream ran; but here the drift was tremendous, and it was with the utmost difficulty that we got to the water's edge. When there, we were fairly puzzled by the changed aspect of everything; but suddenly the evening became lighter, and the drifting snow was not quite so dense. We saw that we should soon be able to ascertain where we were, so we halted for a minute or two, stamping about to keep ourselves from freezing. My poor dog immediately crouched at our feet, and curling himself up, laid down; in a few moments he was nearly covered with the snow. But the storm was evidently ceasing, at any rate for a short time, and very soon a small bit of blue sky appeared overhead, but in a moment it was again concealed by the flying shower. The next time, however, that the blue sky appeared, it was for a longer period, and the snow entirely ceased, allowing us to see our exact position; indeed we were very nearly opposite the house, and within half a mile of it. The river had to be crossed, and it was impossible to find the stepping-stones; but no time was to be lost, as a fresh drift began to appear to windward; so in we went, and dashed through the stream, which was not much above knee-deep, excepting in certain spots, which we contrived to avoid. The poor dog was most unwilling at first to rise from his resting-place, but followed us well when once up. We soon made our way to the house, and got there just as another storm came on, which lasted till after dark, and through which, in our tired state, we never could have made our way. Donald and the shepherd's family were in a state of great anxiety about us, knowing that there would have been no possible means of affording us assistance, had we been bewildered or wearied out upon the mountain. The shepherd himself was fairly knocked up, and could scarcely be prevailed upon to take either food or drink, or even to put off his frozen clothes, before flinging himself on his bed. For my own part, I soon became as comfortable as possible, and slept as soundly and dreamlessly as such exercise only can make one do. I must candidly confess, however, that I made an inward vow against Ptarmigan-shooting again upon snow-covered mountains."

The Ptarmigan is readily taken by snares, and a curious habit which it has, in common with many other birds, of running alongside of any little obstacle instead of leaping over it, has been taken advantage of to ensure its capture in some countries. In Lapland it is said that the inhabitants take them in large numbers, by making little hedges of birch boughs, with openings at intervals, in each of which is placed a snare. The birds come up to feed on the catkins of the birch, run along the hedge, attempt to go through the openings, and are taken in the snares.

"Their flesh is much esteemed," says Daniel, "by the Europeans at Hudson's Bay. They are as tame as chickens, especially in a mild day (in winter); in their wildest state, by being driven about and fired at with powder, they grow so weary by those short flights as very soon to be tame. If the hunters see the birds unexpectedly likely to take a long flight, they imitate the crying of a Hawk, which so greatly intimidates them that they instantly settle. Nets, twenty feet square, fixed to four poles, and supported in front in a perpendicular direction with sticks, is the usual mode adopted to take them; a long line is made fast to these props, the end of which a person holds, who lies concealed at a distance; several people are then employed to drive the birds within reach of the net, which, when pulled down, often covers fifty or sixty. At this time so plentiful are they that ten thousand are taken for the use of the settlement, from November to the end of April.

The time of pairing is, like the other Grouse, early in the spring, and incubation is mostly completed by the beginning or middle of June.

The nest is of the simplest kind, and hardly deserves the name. It consists merely of a slight depression in the ground, with a few scanty twigs or bits of grass and sedge. It is generally by no means easy to be found; for placed, as it often is, under some stone, or plant of heath, it is commonly left by the female as soon as she observes any one approaching, which from the nature of the situation she can readily do; and you thus have but little clue to guide you to where she has deposited her eggs. The eggs, which vary in number from eight or ten to fourteen or fifteen, have a ground colour of yellowish or greenish white, slightly blotched and spotted with dark brown. They are one inch and seven or eight lines in length, by one inch and one or two lines in breadth.

Incubation is completed in twenty-one days, and is performed by the female alone; but the cock bird continues near his partner, perched on some rock or stone, and is said on such occasions to allow himself to be repeatedly pelted with stones.

Like the Red Grouse, the male Ptarmigan assists the female in leading about and protecting the young birds, and they continue together until the following spring, for they cannot be considered to have separated when several broods have united into one large pack.

As soon as the young leave the shell they are able to run about, and are described as being extremely clever and quick in hiding themselves when disturbed. Macgillivray says: "On the summit of one of the Harris mountains, I once happened to stroll into the midst of a covey of very young Ptarmigans, which instantly scattered, and in a few seconds disappeared among the stones, while the mother ran about within a few yards of me, manifesting the most intense anxiety, and pretending to be unable to fly. She succeeded so effectually in drawing my attention to herself, that when I at length began to search for the young, not one of them could be found, although the place was so bare that one might have supposed it impossible for them to escape detection."

The Ptarmigan is most difficult to keep in confinement for any length of time, and has never been known to breed, except in a state of nature.

The adult male in his winter dress has the bill brownish black; a band or streak past the eye, black; irides, yellow brown; over each eye is a semi-lunar patch of bright scarlet naked skin. Shafts of the quills and all the lateral tail feathers, black; the whole of the rest of the plumage is pure white. Claws, the same colour as the bill, but with the tips and edges horn-colour; toes, feathered to the claws.

The adult female in winter differs but slightly from the male. The black streak past the eye is wanting, but the bases of the feathers on that space are black; the superciliary naked red skin is also wanting.

Selby says: "In spring the plumage becomes varied on the upper and under parts with black and deep ochreous yellow; but the quills through all its changes remain white, and their shafts invariably black. Towards autumn the ochreous yellow gives place to a greyish white, and the black spots, which in the spring are large and distinct, become broken, and assume the appearance of zigzag lines and specks. These again, as the season advances, give place to the pure immaculate plumage which distinguishes both sexes during winter."

In the young the feathers are spotted and barred with yellow and dark brown. Wings, white; shafts of quills, dusky; tail, brown black; centre feathers barred with yellow and dark grey.

The weight of the Ptarmigan is about nineteen or twenty ounces.

In length the Ptarmigan will measure from fourteen inches to fifteen and a half, the males being rather the largest.

The *Lagopus rupestris*, or Rock Ptarmigan, which by some

writers is regarded as only a variety of the ordinary species, is said to have occurred in Sutherland and Perthshire. It habitually inhabits arctic America, and Siberia, and Iceland.

As a bird for the table, the Ptarmigan is much inferior to the Red Grouse, being drier and with less flavour; still it is by no means to be despised, and when Moor Game cannot be had, may fairly be called upon to act as its substitute.

BIBLIOGRAPHY.

MACGILLIVRAY'S "British Birds" contains a most accurate and detailed account of the change of the plumage of this bird during the four seasons of the year.

DRESSER, in his "Birds of Europe," gives an admirable account of its distribution throughout Northern Europe and Asia and on the more elevated mountain ranges of Southern Europe, with representations of the species in its various stages of plumage.

BOOTH'S "Rough Notes on the Birds of the British Islands" gives admirable illustrations of the bird in summer, autumn, and winter plumage, describing most graphically the difficulties of shooting them on the snow-covered mountains.

PALLAS'S SAND GROUSE

Syrrhaptes paradoxus, ... PALLAS.

Syrrhaptes—One that sews or stitches together (from the union of
  the toes).
Paradoxus—Paradoxical (from the curious structure of the feet).

Syrrhapte paradoxal, French; *Fausthuhn*, German; *Steppehöne*, Danish.

PALLAS'S Sand Grouse is a native of the sandy plains
of Central Asia, of which the great desert of Gobi and
the Kirghis Steppes may be taken as examples. It differs
so essentially from the other and better known Sand Grouse
which are known to naturalists under the name of *Pterocles*
that it has been made the type of a new genus, *Syrrhaptes*,
from συρράπτεω, to sew together, because the toes, except the
last joints, are firmly united. This singular bird has long
been known. Professor Newton regards it as the 'Barquerlac'
of Marco Polo, and the 'Loung-kio' or Dragon's Foot of the
Abbé Huc, so unscientifically described by him in his *Souvenir
d'un Voyage dans la Tartare*, i. p. 244.

The most recent detailed account of the habits of the
Pallas's Sand Grouse in its native steppes is that given by
the celebrated Russian traveller, the late Col. Prjevalski. The
Syrrhaptes paradoxus, he informs us, is one of the most
characteristic birds of Mongolia. In summer they migrate
north even beyond Lake Baikal, where they breed, but spend
the winter in the Gobi desert, in such localities as are free from
snow, and in the middle of October may be met with there,
sometimes in flocks of several thousands.

The principal food of these enormous flocks consists of

the seeds of *Agriophyllum gobicum*, a plant allied to our common goosefoot or wild spinach (*Chenopodium*).

Their flight is very fast, the wings making a peculiar noise; and when a large flock is on the wing, it can be heard from a considerable distance, the noise somewhat resembling the sighing of the wind. When in the air the male birds often utter a peculiar note, something like '*truck - turuck, truck-turuck.*'

At the feeding - place the whole flock sits closely, and, having formed a line, run forward very clumsily and slowly, taking short steps and waddling from side to side. The tracks which they leave on the ground very much resemble those of some small mammals, and cover, in endless series, the sandy deserts.

The Sand Grouse does not construct a nest at all, but deposits its eggs on the sand, sometimes without even making a hole; occasionally, however, a few grass blades are used as a lining. The eggs are remarkable for their regular elliptical shape, and are marked with reddish and brownish spots and streaks on a dirty yellowish grey ground.

This Sand Grouse is very cautious and shy, though scarcely pursued by man at all; and although its plumage is very much like the ground of the desert, the bird does not trust to that when in danger, but tries to escape by flight, rising before one can get within gun-shot, and very seldom alights again in the immediate neighbourhood. Henderson's falcon is the only bird of prey that persecutes them; but even he cannot always catch them, as they are very quick.

The late Consul Swinhoe describes their migration to China in severe winters, and says: "Flocks of hundreds constantly pass over with a very swift flight, not unlike that of the Golden Plover, for which we at first mistook them. The market at Tientsin was literally glutted with them, and you could purchase them for a mere nothing. The natives called them *Sha-chee* or Sand Fowl, and told me they were mostly caught in clap-nets."

The food of the Pallas's Sand Grouse in its native habitat

has been already described by the observers quoted.   The crops of the specimens killed in England have shown a very large preponderance of the seeds of weeds over those of cultivated plants.   Mr. Tegetmeier writes: "One specimen that I have had under my notice contained many hundreds of the seeds of the common chickweed (*Stellaria media*).   I have also found the seeds of that almost universally distributed grass (*Poa annua*) in the crops of many."

The general colour of the plumage may be described as sandy or ochreous, barred with brown and black; the sides of the neck and throat are orange; there is a narrow band of black-edged feathers on the breast, and a second broader and darker band on the flanks and across the abdomen; the back, scapular feathers, and upper tail coverts are marked with black and dark brown bars.   The primary wing or quill feathers are delicate lavender with dark tips; they are unusually pointed, especially the first, which is the longest, extending far beyond the others, and giving the wing its remarkably pointed form. The tail is formed of sixteen feathers, the central pair of which are most remarkable, as they become elongated into mere pointed filaments at the tips, and extend in the males at least three inches beyond the others.   The total length of the male, from the beak to the extreme point of the tail, exceeds fifteen inches.   The weight of the birds when in good condition is from ten and a half to eleven ounces.   The female is somewhat smaller, and is generally duller in colour, without the golden orange on the neck, which is marked with black; the chest band is very indistinct, and the central feathers of the tail less elongated.

The legs in both sexes are very short, and closely covered with buffish white feathers down to the toes.   The feet are so exceptional in structure that it may not be without interest to describe them somewhat in detail.

In the ordinary Sand Grouse, constituting the genus *Pterocles*, of which different species are found in the South of Europe, North Africa, Senegal, Arabia, India, &c., the feet do not differ essentially in structure from those of other

allied birds. But in Pallas's Sand Grouse, and in the closely
related larger bird from Tibet which was subsequently discovered, the feet are so peculiarly constructed that Illiger
placed the former in a separate genus, to which he gave
the name *Syrrhaptes*, to signify that the toes were bound
together; and he retained Pallas's specific name *Paradoxus*,
from the strange, paradoxical structure of the feet. This
singular formation is not so visible from the front; the short
tarsus and upper surface of the foot being equally covered
with short close feathers, from which the three blunt claws
protrude. In looking at the under side or sole of the foot,

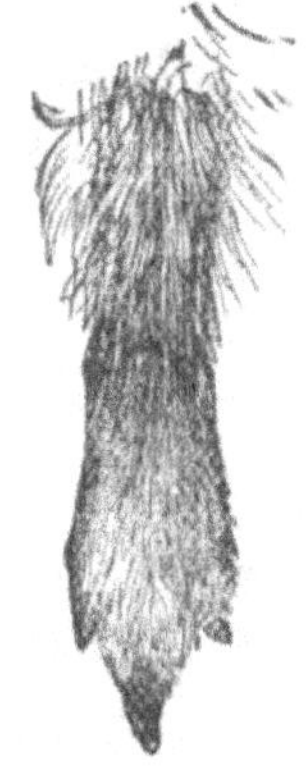

FIG. 1.—*Upper Surface.*

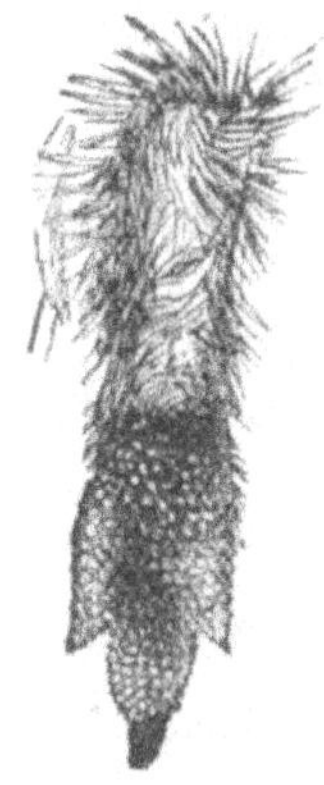

FIG. 2.—*Under Surface.*

FOOT OF PALLAS'S SAND GROUSE.

as shown in the second figure, it will be seen that the tarsus
is feathered below, but that the toes are connected together
by a leathery pad, the surface of which is covered by small
circular warty prominences, closely packed together. The hind
toe is entirely wanting.

This peculiar structure, which is accurately shown in the
woodcuts that were most carefully drawn and engraved from
fresh specimens, will serve at once to distinguish Pallas's Sand
Grouse from any other bird to be met with in Great Britain.

The shortness of the legs causes the birds to move in

an exceptional manner when on the ground, proceeding with a waddling gait, swaying from side to side as they proceed.

The affinities of the Sand Grouse are remarkable and very distinctive. From the Pigeons, which they closely resemble in many respects, they differ in the young, being thickly covered with down, and able to shift for themselves; and in the nest containing three eggs, which are of a dull olive, with darker brown spots, so as to be well protected from observation when laid on the bare sand; whereas the eggs of the Pigeons are never more than two in number, and white. The hind toe, which is always present in Pigeons and Fowls, is wanting. The gall-bladder, which is absent in most of the Pigeons, is present in the Sand Grouse; and they also have very large lower intestines or cœca, like the Fowls. In their habits they differ much from the Pigeons, drinking in the ordinary manner, and flying, like the Plover, without any gliding motion on outspread wings, such as may often be noticed in flights of Pigeons. The mode of feeding the young has not been carefully described; but I should surmise that the latter pick up seeds for themselves from the first, and are not fed with curd-like secretions from the crops of the parents, as in all the Columbine family. In the arrangement of their muscles, and in the structure of the skeleton, they offer several peculiarities. The sternum or breast-bone is remarkable for the extreme depth of the keel, especially at the front; this indicates the existence of powerful pectoral muscles, and gives rise to a singular habit which the bird has of lying on its side, even, it is said, when incubating. The furculum or merry-thought bone is remarkable for its small development in comparison with the size of the sternum. As in the common Grouse and many other allied birds, the flesh on the breast is of two colours. The outer layer, which is dark, is the great pectoral muscle, which by its vigorous contraction pulls the wing down and causes it to strike the air, and support and propel the bird. The lower white muscle is the smaller pectoral, the tendon or cord from which passes over the bone as over a pulley, and by its contraction raises the wing for a second stroke. Why in the Sand Grouse and some other birds these two muscles— known to anatomists as the pectoralis major and minor respectively—should be of different colours and texture, whilst in the majority of birds, even those as swift in flight, they should not differ, is one of those secrets of nature that have yet to be disclosed.

Differing as the Sand Grouse do from the birds of every other group, although allied most closely to the Pigeons, the Grouse, and the Plovers, most naturalists have agreed to form them into a separate group which includes only two genera—*Pterocles*, the ordinary Sand Grouse, of which about a dozen distinct species are known, inhabiting Asia, Africa, and part of Europe, none of which have ever been found in England; and the solid-footed birds, *Syrrhaptes*, of which Pallas's Sand Grouse, *S. paradoxus*, is the type, and of which only one other species, *S. tibetanus*, is known.

There have been two great migrations of this singular bird from the plains of Tartary to the extreme west of Europe, and occasionally single birds or pairs have appeared at other times. The first great invasion, however, was in 1863, when flocks appeared in many parts of our country, extending from the extreme north to south Devon, and going as far west as Donegal. Professor Newton estimated that no less than 700 visited our Islands at that date. The second migration occurred in 1888, and consisted of much larger numbers; flocks of birds, thirty, forty, and more, were seen in various parts of Great Britain. They were unfortunately mostly shot and not allowed to increase in numbers. They, however, in some instances nested, and hatched their young; but they were not protected, being slain down without mercy, and it is doubtful whether a single specimen now exists in Western Europe.

Pallas's Sand Grouse formed a prominent feature at the public dinner of the now-defunct Acclimatization Society in 1863. During the second visitation large numbers were shot and used for food, many being even sold in the country markets.   As culinary birds they are satisfactory, though by no means of first-rate excellence.

BIBLIOGRAPHY.

THE following is a list of works which may be consulted for further information relating to this species :—

MOORE, T. J.   *The Ibis*, 1860.   Detailed account, with coloured plate by Wolf, of the first appearance in England in July 1859.

NEWTON, Prof. ALFRED.   " Proc. Zool. Society," 1861.   Describes the structure, and points out how the Sand Grouse differ from the *Columbidæ* and the true *Gallinæ*.   The egg of the species is described from a specimen laid in the Zoological Society's Gardens, and figured for the first time.   And in *The Ibis* for 1864, Prof. Newton gives a detailed history of the irruption of 1863, with map showing localities in which it was noticed in Europe.

DRESSER, H. E.   " Birds of Europe," Vol. VII.   The most detailed history of the occurrence of the species on the Continent, with account of its habits in Asia, as given by Prjevalski, Radde, and Swinhoe; with coloured figures by Keulemans.

SAUNDERS, HOWARD, in " Yarrell's British Birds," Vol. III., gives the most complete account of the species that is to be found in any work on British birds ; with woodcuts of birds and of sternum.

GOULD, J., in " Birds of Great Britain," gives a figure which is not satisfactory, and many of the details of the text are erroneous.

STEVENSON, H.   " The Birds of Norfolk."   An admirable account of the species as observed in Norfolk at the period of the irruption of 1863; with coloured plate by Wolf.

TEGETMEIER, W. B.   " Pallas's Sand Grouse."   Gives the natural history of the species; with coloured plate and woodcuts.   Out of print.

MACPHERSON, Rev. H. A.   " The Visitation of Pallas's Sand Grouse."   Contains an account of its distribution in Scotland in 1888.

THE PARTRIDGE

COMMON PARTRIDGE—GREY PARTRIDGE.

Perdix cinerea, ... LATHAM.

Perdix—A Partridge, in classical authors. *Cinerea*—Ash-coloured, or grey.

Perdrix grise, French; *Starna,* Italian; *Rebhuhn, Feldhuhn,* German; *Patrijs, Veldhoen,* Dutch; *Almindelig, Agerhöne,* Danish; *Raphöne,* Norwegian, *Åkerhöna,* Swedish; *Turkinpyy, Peltopyy,* Finnish; *Kouropatka,* Russian.

PERHAPS scarcely any other Game Bird is better known in this country, or is, on the whole, more deserving of the esteem in which it is held, than the Partridge. Selecting, as it does by choice, the most highly cultivated parts of the country for its resort, it offers to the sportsman, almost at his own door, most agreeable shooting, without the extreme labour and separation from his family and friends which is the penalty paid by the Grouse-shooter for his more exciting pleasures. It is an interesting fact in the history of this bird, that while the extension of cultivation has gradually diminished the numbers of some birds, and has entirely banished others from districts where formerly they were in abundance, the direct contrary effect has resulted in the case of the Partridge, which we find to increase most abundantly in those localities where the modern system of farming is carried to its greatest extent. Being an indigenous inhabitant of these Islands, the Partridge only requires fair play to increase and multiply to almost any desired extent.

In speaking of the distribution of this bird over the country, we shall only state that it occurs in more or less abundance wherever moderate protection is afforded to it, except on those wild and rude moors and wastes which we have described as the peculiar haunts of the Grouse; and yet we have the authority of Mr. St. John for the fact, that in Sutherland he has occasionally met with it in situations usually resorted to by the Red Grouse alone. Confirmatory of this, and also as adding to our knowledge of the economy of the bird, we quote the following from a letter from Mr. George Jackson, keeper to Lord Bantry at Glengariff:—"In this very mountainous district (the country between Bantry Bay and the Bay of Kenmare), I frequently find coveys far distant from any cultivated land. Curiosity caused me to examine what they fed on, and I found in their stomachs some seeds of a coarse kind of grass indigenous to the place, some kind of green herbage, and a quantity of spiders that are numerous among the heath."

In Ireland this bird, although very generally distributed, appears to be found in much less abundance than in England, and, from some unexplained cause, seems to have greatly diminished in numbers of late years. Mr. Thompson, in his "Natural History of Ireland," has entered pretty fully into the supposed causes of this decrease; but as yet nothing positive has been proved. Mr. Thompson has mentioned the following among other believed injurious influences, namely, the prevalence of the custom of pickling seed wheat in poisonous solutions, to prevent the ravages of wire-worms, &c. As this is a matter of great importance, not only in Ireland but also in England, we give the following as quoted by Mr. Thompson, from a communication of Dr. H. W. Fuller, of St. George's Hospital, to *The Lancet*:—

"'In Hampshire, Partridges have been found dead in the fields, presenting a very remarkable appearance. Instead of lying prostrate on their sides, as is usually the case with dead birds, they have been found sitting with their heads erect, and their eyes open, presenting all the semblance of life. This peculiarity, which for some time had attracted considerable attention among sportsmen in the neighbourhood, led to no practical result until a covey of ten birds having been found nestled together in this condition, two of the birds, together with the seeds taken from the crops of the remaining eight, were sent up to London for examination.' On analysis, Dr. Fuller discovered considerable quantities of arsenic in the viscera of the birds; this was traced to the seed corn in their crops. Inquiry established that in many parts of the country the farmers were in the habit of steeping their wheat in a strong solution of arsenic, previous to sowing it, with the view of preventing the ravages of the wire-worm on the seed, and of the smut on the plant when grown; this process is found to be successful, and is frequently adopted; the seed is poisonous when sown, but the grain produced is in no degree affected by the poison; wherever this plan has been extensively carried out, Pheasants and Partridges have been poisoned by eating the seed, and the Partridges have been almost invariably found sitting in the position already described; the men employed in sowing the poisonous seed not unfrequently present the earlier symptoms which occur in the milder cases of poisoning by arsenic.

"The question was then suggested, 'Might not the flesh of birds so poisoned prove injurious when eaten?' Dr. Fuller cut off the breast of a bird, and gave it to a healthy cat; she ate it with avidity; but in about half-an-hour she began to vomit, and vomited almost incessantly for nearly twelve hours, during the whole of which time she evidently suffered excessive pain. Dr. Fuller also found in every part of the flesh traces of arsenic; the bird could not have been eaten by a man without very serious consequences. 'It is notorious,' says Dr. Fuller, 'that many of the dealers in game are supplied through the agency of poachers and others, who have a direct pecuniary interest in supplying them with the largest possible number of birds. It is certain, moreover, that if men of this sort were to find a covey of Partridges in a field, dead, but fresh and in good condition, they would not hesitate to send them, with the remainder of their booty, to the poulterer, who would, as certainly without suspicion, sell them to his customers.'"

The facts here detailed are of great importance, not alone to the sportsman, but also to all who eat bought Partridges at the season when wheat is sown.

The flesh of the Partridge is delicately flavoured, and although other Game Birds are objected to by some individuals, it is rare to see any one refuse to partake of this excellent bird; indeed the general good qualities of the Partridge as a bird for the table are almost proverbial, and gave rise to the old couplet—

> "If the Partridge had the Woodcock's thigh,
> 'Twould be the best bird that e'er did fly."

The habits of the Partridge lead it to frequent the more open cultivated parts of the country; it is especially fond of corn-fields while the plant is growing, for there it has ample shelter; and after the corn is cut it picks up a good deal of its food in the stubbles, thereby rendering the farmer good service. The modern practice of mowing the wheat leaves a much shorter stubble, and consequently less cover for the birds. Wheat stubbles are preferred by them to barley stubbles; though these latter are by no means despised. The colour of the Partridge assimilating so closely as it does to that of a stubble-field, they readily secrete themselves, even in large coveys, in the furrows and behind clods. During the time of harvest, when the corn-fields are full of men and horses, they resort to the neighbouring fields, returning to feed in the evening, and also in the early morning, to the corn-fields. In the winter, when the stubbles are ploughed up, they betake themselves more to the rough meadows, where clumps of grass and mole-hills exist. Potato-fields and turnips are also very favourite resorts, and they may very frequently be found in them when not feeding in the stubbles. They will even be found sometimes in copses where there is underwood of brambles, fern, and coarse grass. Unless greatly disturbed, coveys will keep pretty nearly to the same localities, whether for feeding or resting, and hiding.

The Partridge never perches on trees, being essentially a ground bird. It runs with great velocity; but when suddenly alarmed, it usually either squats very close, or else flies off at once. Its flight is tolerably quick, and must be familiar to most people. After rising to a moderate height, which it does in an oblique, and not in a perpendicular direction, it at once makes off in a straight course, quickly flapping its wings, which produces a sound well known to every sportsman, and which may be compared to the word 'whirr,' with the 'r' indefinitely prolonged, as whirr-r-r-r-r-r-r. During its flight it will occasionally, and particularly towards its termination, cease flapping its wings, and sail on with steady pinions for some distance, ending at last in a sidelong manner.

During the winter months Partridges will sometimes, especially in wild districts, pack like Grouse. We remember while shooting at Hatfield, in Lincolnshire, seeing a pack of about forty; they were extremely wild and wary. It was said not to be an uncommon occurrence in that district, though at that time we were unaware that Partridges ever congregated in winter in greater numbers than an ordinary covey, or double covey, which is sometimes found where two pairs have nested close together, and the young birds have got mingled, and remained with one pair. Packing, however, is rare in most districts, particularly where small enclosures prevail.

The Partridge is very fond of basking and sunning itself during the middle of the day in warm and sheltered situations, such as on the sunny side of a hedge bank; and like other gallinaceous birds, it frequently dusts itself, as we see Sparrows do in the dry and dusty roads.

After leaving the feeding-ground at dusk for their roosting-places, which are very frequently grass-fields, the covey first separates, and runs over a considerable space of ground, as if to ascertain that all is safe and quiet; the old cock may be heard as if directing these movements; and when the ground has been sufficiently examined, he calls them to him, and they pass the night all close together, arranged in a circle, with their heads to the outside.

Mr. Thompson mentions a very curious circumstance with respect to the Partridge, which it is difficult to account for. He says, "There is a singular difference in habit between the Partridge of the North of Ireland and that of the opposite portion of Scotland, as is well known to sportsmen who have shot in both countries: I have myself remarked it with some interest.   An Irish covey generally springs without uttering a call; but the Scotch covey shrieks with all its might when sprung.   The Scotch birds too, even where very little molested, more knowingly take care of themselves than the Irish: their watchfulness is extraordinary.   Their sense of hearing, as well as sight, must be remarkably acute.   One day in the month of October, an experienced sportsman and myself sprang either twenty-four or twenty-six coveys (nearly all double, or containing about two dozen of birds) in the neighbourhood of Ballantrae, when they all not only forbade a near approach, but, though we advanced as silently as possible, never admitted us into the same field with them.   I have known Partridges that, when sprung there, called loudly like old cock birds, prove, on being shot, young birds of the year."

Their call note on these occasions has been likened by Meyer to the words 'chisick, chisick.'

The Partridge is strictly monogamous, and when pairing has once taken place, it is truly "to love and to cherish, till death do us part."

Partridges, when placed under certain unusual circumstances, appear sometimes to lose entirely their presence of mind, if one may so term their attempts at self-preservation; in illustration of this we quote the following, as recorded in *The Naturalist*, by Mr. John Williamson, Jun., of Emanuel College, Cambridge:—"At the Newmarket Houghton meeting on the 29th of October (1852), and during the racing, a covey of seven Partridges flew across the Heath to the poles near the betting-stand. When they found they could not alight in consequence of the number of carriages and spectators, they continued their course, and alighted within two hundred yards of the stand, and on the bare course. One of the birds, separating from the rest, wheeled back over the heads of the mob, and by one of them was ultimately caught. Encouraged by this strange capture, many persons ran to the spot where the remainder had been marked, and after a series of running chases, the whole number were secured. Only one bird attempted a flight, but, alarmed at its pursuers, it dropped after rising about two yards, and the whole covey were secured."

Mr. Daniel mentions a still more singular fact :—" In Blickling Park, Norfolk, during the races there, at the very height of the sport, a covey of Partridges sprung up, and were flying across the ground, when, overcome with alarm at the noise and bustle of the scene, they fell among the throng, and were picked up by some of the spectators."

Another equally curious circumstance is also related by him :—" A covey of sixteen Partridges were disturbed by some men at plough, and directed their flight across the cliff to the sea, over which they continued their course about three hundred yards, when the whole were observed to drop into the water. Twelve of them were soon after floated to shore by the tide, and picked up by a boy, who carried them to Eastbourne, where he disposed of his birds at ninepence each ! "

That the Partridge may be tamed and will become extremely familiar has often been proved; but we never remember reading a more interesting account than the following by Mr. Arthur Hussey, of Rottingdean, which we extract from the *Zoologist*. The account was written by a lady who was the owner and trainer of birds :—" On the 5th of July 1839, I received a small hamper, containing a parcel of cotton wool, in the midst of which was a young Partridge, about a day old. The little wild thing could not be induced to eat, so I was obliged to feed it with boiled rice. I never expected to bring it up, having always heard that to handle a Partridge was a sure way to destroy it; but there is no rule without an exception, and this little creature was hardly ever out of my hands. It soon became quite tame, and whenever I put my hands together before it, it would creep in, and go to sleep very well contented. Warmth being indispensable, I used to pin it up in a fleecy-hosiery for the night, and in the morning fed it quite early, leaving it to sleep again.

"Rice, bread, and ants' eggs were its food, upon which it thrived. It soon showed it liked to be always with me, and was perfectly happy in my lap; or when I have been painting, it would sit on my left arm, dressing itself, or sleeping in entire security. When it outgrew the flannel, and I could no longer have it pinned up, I used to take it into my mother's room, and if it could lie on her gown at her feet it was contented, but was always on the watch for my coming back, and on seeing me, would jump up and run to meet me. It was now so tame and pleased with being fondled as to excite much astonishment. My mother soon became very fond of it, and by degrees it was more with her than with me. Its cage was never inhabited; it would never sleep in confinement, therefore was awake and quite alive all the evening, being either in the lap or on the sofa.

"When he had changed his feathers, and attained his full plumage, he refused to be handled; but his habits were just as sociable as before. His knowledge of every one was most extraordinary; his likings and dislikings were very strong; and he was so curious and observant that no piece of furniture could be removed without his finding it out; and if the carpet was not smooth, he would set to work instantly to render it so, by scratching and pecking. He was very fond of gay colours, and no new gown or cap could be put on without catching his attention. He never offered to go up stairs or down, and very rarely used his wings;

on being gently chastised when he did fly, he would run and hide himself like a child, as if he knew he had done wrong.

"A box of earth was given him to rub in, which he thoroughly enjoyed. His feathers were always glossy and in the most perfect order, which I attribute to his always having plenty of green food, such as grass and clover cut small. In the winter he liked wheat, but rarely touched it in the summer; was very fond of sugar and cake; drank very little water, and liked his food dry. He never forgot any one he had made acquaintance with, and the return of any of the family after many months' absence caused him so much joy and excitement that I have been compelled to shut him up. He would distinguish the voices, even before they got out of the carriage. His partiality for my mother was very great, and if she was asleep, nothing would tempt him to quit her; but he never liked her to be in the drawing-room. In the evening he always came into the drawing-room, and remained till we retired. He slept at my bedside, and never disturbed me, nor got up himself till I was called; and then he had a particular call if he fancied I was gone to sleep again. Once, from being frightened, he flew out of the window, and being recovered after much trouble (it was in a town), he never again offered to get out. After this we had nets at the windows; and the net being one day left down in my room, by running up to my mother, and then into my room, he attracted her notice, and she followed him, he standing before the window, and when the net was replaced, showing himself satisfied. Unlike most pets, he died a natural death on the 1st of January 1843."

Another instance of this kind is related by Daniel, who says, "Amongst the very few instances of the Partridge remaining tame, was that of one which had been reared at the Rev. Mr. Bird's: this, long after its full growth, attended the parlour at breakfast and other times, received food from any hand that would condescend to give it, stretched itself before, and seemed much to enjoy the warmth of the fire, and at length fell a victim to the decided foe of all favourite birds, a cat: his dogs were too generous to molest it."

These, however, are but rare cases, and more commonly the home-reared Partridge, on acquiring maturity, gradually also acquires its natural wildness, and seeks the more congenial atmosphere of the fields.

That the Partridge will sometimes, under the influence of sudden surprise, feign death, would appear from the following incident, related by Mr. J. J. Briggs, of Melbourne, Derbyshire:—"February 18th, 1844: I was riding along a field, and came suddenly upon a Partridge; it did not rise with a whirring noise, and wing its way out of danger, but ran a few feet upon the turf, which was very bare, and squatted down suddenly, lying as close as a hare on her seat: its head touched the grass, and its neck was stretched out, as if it were a dead bird. I rode up to it quite close, but it moved not a feather, and I could scarcely make it escape although I cracked my whip; it was not disabled, for when it did rise it flew strong and well, and my impression was that it was feigning to be a dead bird."

The following extraordinary instance of courage in the Partridge, or whatever it may be called, is recorded by Aubrey as having been mentioned by Charles the First. He says that when he was a Freshman at Oxford in 1642, he often went to see Charles the First, who then resided at the university, at supper: on one of these occasions he heard him say, "That as he was hawking in Scotland, he rode into the Quarry, and found the covey of Partridges falling upon the Hawk;" and he adds that the Monarch said, "I will swear upon the Book that it is true."

Partridges are taken by poachers very readily, and in wholesale numbers, by means of a kind of drag net, which, however, does not drag on the ground, but is carried by four men, one at each corner, just enough off the ground to escape the bushes placed on the grass-fields to embarrass the poacher; several bullets are attached to the net at different parts by cords, just long enough to allow them to touch the

ground. The bullets are sure to disturb the birds, and as
soon as the poachers hear their flutterings they instantly
drop the net, and thus frequently capture the whole covey.
Poachers, however, are cunning fellows, and the following
ingenious improvement upon this, the ordinary method, is
mentioned by Meyer :—"For taking of Partridges, a singular
method has been adopted by some poachers, namely, to pro-
vide a setting dog, upon the head of which they fix a lantern,
for the purpose of his ranging the field at night : on his
stopping, the poachers know where the Partridges lie, and
draw the net up to him accordingly. The gamekeepers of
the Earl of Carlisle, some time since (now about twenty
years ago), being on their nightly perambulations, were not
a little astonished and alarmed at seeing a light traversing
the field in a very singular manner ; they prepared their
guns accordingly, and in a short time the light made a sudden
stop, when three or four men, whom they had not descried,
making their appearance, they were secured in the act of
drawing a large net up to the light upon the head of the
setter, as above mentioned."

Partridges are usually poached by some such method as
above mentioned ; the gun is seldom or never used except
by the sporting poacher—a very different character from the
ordinary poacher, for he follows the game from the love of
sporting, and not merely for the money value of the birds.

In addition to the poacher, the Partridge has other, what
may be called, natural enemies, by which it suffers much,
particularly in the young state. Among these may be named
the Carrion Crow ; the Stoat or Ermine ; the Fox ; Hawks
of various kinds ; and lastly, the Adder or Viper (*Pelius
berus*), which is more frequently guilty of destroying young
Partridges than is commonly supposed.

The food of the Partridge varies at different seasons of
the year ; thus we find it in winter, spring, and summer feeding chiefly on blades and seeds of grass, seeds of various
species of *Polygonum*, and many other weeds ; and very
largely of insects of all kinds and in all stages of develop-

ment. Among others, it seeks diligently for wire-worms, so destructive to the growing crops; also for aphides, spiders, ants, and their eggs; and in fact for every insect that frequents its haunts; thereby doing an incalculable amount of good to the farmer, who, for his own sake, should do all in his power to protect and encourage this most useful bird.

During the autumn they derive a portion of their nutriment from the corn-fields; but we believe they never pull growing corn: the amount of corn consumed by them before the crop is carried off the ground can be but trifling, and any that they may pick up after that from the stubbles must be looked upon as entailing, not only no loss, but a positive benefit on the agriculturist; for all grains left to vegetate, and grow up among any other crops, can only be looked upon as injurious weeds by every good farmer. During this period also they destroy large numbers of insects, which are generally then very abundant. The young birds subsist almost wholly upon insect food, and take but a very small portion of corn. Along with its vegetable food, like the rest of the *Gallinaceæ*, the Partridge always swallows a number of small hard stones, seldom exceeding a No. 2 shot in size; these assist the gizzard in grinding up the food and preparing it for assimilation.

It is stated by Mr. Yarrell, "that on some heathy districts in Surrey, as the Hurtwood and Bagshot Heaths, the Partridges seldom frequent the corn-lands, but subsist on heath and hurtle-berries. These birds are not so white in the flesh when dressed as others, and have some of the flavour of the Grouse."

An instance is on record, by Mr. Daniel, of a Partridge having been shot near Newbury, in October 1807, which on being opened was found to have swallowed a Viper (*Pelius berus*), thirteen inches long.

One family of Partridges is called by sportsmen a covey. You spring Partridges when you put them up; you shoot a brace or a brace and a half of birds. The foot-marks of the Partridge are called its rode. Their sleeping is called jucking, or jugging.

The Partridge is one of the most valued Game Birds, and is therefore everywhere carefully preserved. The old method of shooting over dogs is now, comparatively speaking, but little followed, owing to the great alteration in the mode of agriculture that has taken place during the last twenty years. Referring to this, Mr. Stevenson writes as follows:—"That those who were accustomed in the 'good old days' to kill Partridges after this fashion, more especially since the chief enjoyment of that time consisted in watching and profiting by the sagacity of the dogs, should regard the present system with but little favour, is natural enough; but why sneer at the taste of younger men who have adopted from necessity, and not from choice, the shooting *en battue* of the last twenty years? What sport, I would ask, with even the best trained dogs, would be afforded now on our closely mown stubbles? or, beyond a few 'points' here and there in a large field of turnips, what chance of a bag, when the birds, once alarmed, commence running in all directions along the open drills? There is but little harbour in our highly cultivated lands; and the trimmed fences in many places afford scarcely shelter enough for a wounded bird. 'The four-course' system also, though a fine institution for farming purposes, often puts the sportsman to much difficulty, his success depending greatly on the position of the crops—a very common answer to inquiries on any Partridge farm at the commencement of the season being, 'We have plenty of birds, but the turnips lie so awkward this year.' Under these circumstances, then, the gunners have but little chance of sport, except by walking in line with the beaters; and unquestionably there is no comparison between the difficulty of such shooting and that under the old system, as the birds rise unexpectedly and at uncertain distances. By this method, now universally adopted both in the enclosed and more exposed portions of the country, very fine shooting is obtained on the wide open heath-lands in the western and south-western districts, when the birds, bred on the adjacent corn-lands, are either found basking on the outskirts, or are driven on from the neighbouring stubbles.

"The guns and beaters, advancing in line, drive the game forward into the nearest coverts; and here and there, though often at long intervals, thick belts of gorse and broom offer a fatal shelter to the birds, and a hot fusillade and a rapid addition to the bag repay the toil of the sportsman. Later in the season, however, when the birds become 'packed,' as it is termed (large coveys consorting together for mutual safety), the 'driving' system before referred to is now commonly adopted for both English and French birds. This is certainly the perfection of sport for those possessed of the necessary quickness and skill; but to the uninitiated, at least, it is nervous work, standing under shelter of a fence or a loft of hurdles drawn with gorse, and peering anxiously through the prickly screen to watch the motions of the driving party. Coveys and single birds are marked down at different points; and presently the beaters, spreading out in line, are coming on. Now is the time! Never mind that noisy heart of yours, that will thump, thump, like an eight-day clock. Keep your eyes open, grip your gun-stock tight. Whish! Here they come! Bang! bang! And the birds, killed high in the air, fall dead some thirty yards behind the gunners. An old hand perhaps bags his brace, though coming at heaven knows what an hour; for the pace of a Partridge thus flushed at a distance is something extra-ordinary. Ask the novice, for instance, after such a flight, if he got a shot that time? 'Shot!—what at? I heard you fire; and something came with a whish past my head; but it was gone before I turned round.' Yet this style of shooting, which to sportsmen of the old school would have appeared an impossibility, is now accomplished with such certainty by the crack shots of the day, that a party of eight guns killed seven hundred and forty-four Partridges, besides one hundred and fifty-seven Hares and sixty Pheasants, in one day, by 'driving,' at Seamer, near Scarborough, as recorded by Mr. Stuart Wortley :—

"It is by no means an unusual circumstance for Partridges when flushed in the vicinity of the telegraph-wires to fly against them in their headlong course. At Larling, where the International telegraph crosses an extensive heath preserved for sporting purposes, I have known as many as six or eight birds thus killed in one day when driven forward by the beaters ; and Mr. Alfred Newton informs me that when shooting at Elevedon, near Thetford, he has seen five birds killed out of a covey in the same way. They are also occasionally found dead under the wires on foggy mornings, but this more particularly in places where the wires have but recently been introduced."

Partridge-shooting is fixed by law to commence on the 1st of September ; but it would be much better if the young birds were allowed a fortnight longer, as indeed they are on many manors with manifest advantage, for the crops are then more generally off the ground, and the birds stronger on the wing.

The following humorous lines appeared in *The Sportsman* magazine for September 1834. Whether they procured the writer the invitations he wished for does not appear.

TO SPORTSMEN.

I've bought a gun,—a powder flask—
   And laid out all my pelf!
But selfish souls won't shoot themselves,
   Nor let me shoot MYSELF !

'Tis true some friend might give a day
   To tranquillise my nerves ;
But save some dainty pots of jam,
   I have no " CHOICE PRESERVES ! "

I seek the sport but now and then—
   I'm none of your encroachers—
Altho' my gun is one of " Egg's,"
   I ne'er encourage " POACHERS ! "

I could not slaughter every hare,
  And yet my maxim's this:
"That married men should always hit—
  They have no right to MISS!"

I'd care not if from lord or duke
  The invitation came—
From 'High—Low—Jack"—or any one,
  So I could get the "GAME!"

Well! here's my hint. I'm quite prepared
  To join a sportsman's banners;
So, Sirs, you'll quickly ask me down—
  If you have any MANNERS!

H. W. C.

The dogs used by sportsmen in the pursuit of the Partridge are either pointers, or setters, or retrievers. Some prefer one kind, some the other. Setters are generally considered to have a finer scent than pointers, and to be capable of enduring more fatigue when they have access to plenty of water.

Several instances have at different times been given of birds which had been shot at, but were actually flying off, suddenly falling to the ground with a wing broken. Mr. A. Hussey has mentioned two such cases in the *Zoologist*, one of which related to a Partridge. Mr. C. St. John has also mentioned the Wild Swan and the Mallard as having fallen to his gun in a similar way. The explanation of this fact is, no doubt, that a single shot had struck the bone of the wing, and either splintered or slightly cracked it, so as to weaken it, but not sufficiently to disable the wing. On the bird using all its powers to escape, the weakened bone gives way, and the poor bird falls to the ground. It cannot, however, be of very frequent occurrence.

At the present time the practice of driving Partridges towards the shooters by means of beaters with flags is largely followed, very large numbers being secured in this way; but even Mr. Stuart Wortley, a strong advocate of the system, writes: "Driving Partridges is the cream, the luxury, and poetry of the sport; walking up is the very marrow and essence of it. I defy any one to handle a line of men, or arrange a beat for driving, who has not plenty of experience in walking after them. The Partridge, like most things, must be known from all points of view, that he may be properly appreciated and dealt with. Walking up, or shooting Partridges over dogs, is, in my judgment, the finest training of all for a young shooter. Here he can learn everything of the habits of the birds, of the instinct or the merits of the dogs, of the faults and failings of the men."

In preserving Partridges, it is absolutely essential that the old cock birds be kept down within proper limits; if this is not the case, the contests for the hens are so violent that incubation is seldom perfected. On this subject Daniel says: "According to Ray, there are one-third more male than female Partridges hatched; and it is well known the old cocks will drive the young off the ground, and afterwards frequently fight until they kill each other. (Partridges, in this respect, differ from Pheasants: they will have a certain range to themselves, whilst Pheasants will hatch and live quietly with their broods close together.) When too many birds are left, these contentions are sure to happen; and the consequence is a scanty produce, for the female is so pursued that she drops her eggs in various places, forming no nest, and perhaps never laying two eggs in the same spot. So well aware was the Duke of Kingston of this circumstance, that he always had the Partridges netted upon his manors as soon as paired, and destroyed all the cocks. The late Mr. Doughty, of Leiston, who was an excellent and most observant sportsman, once preserved an overstock of old Partridges, and declared to the compiler, he did not believe, for two seasons following, there was a covey of young birds upon a tract of near three thousand acres of as fine breeding land as any in the kingdom; he shot and encouraged the destruction of this stock of ancients by all possible means; and the result was that the Partridges bred again as abundantly as formerly."

Partridges begin to pair at the end of February or very early in March; but should the weather prove severe after this, they will sometimes form into coveys again. Like other gallinaceous birds, pairing is not effected without many well-fought battles by the males for the possession of the other sex.

The nest is merely a hollow scraped in the earth, with sometimes a few straws, dead leaves, or blades of grass. It is placed under some tuft of grass or small bush, or in clover, grass, or corn fields. But although these are the more usual situations chosen for the nest, still it is occasionally found in very curious, and one would imagine insecure places. Thus instances are mentioned by Montagu and Daniel where nests were placed in the broad tops of pollard oaks, and the young birds hatched and carried off in security. Frequently, too, the nest may be discovered near to some well-used footpath, and yet the young are very generally reared in these situations, the birds sitting remarkably close, and so escape the eye of the marauding schoolboy. To these may be added the tops of haystacks; and holes in decayed trees or hedgerows, as much as four feet from the ground, as mentioned by Mr. J. M'Intosh, in *The Naturalist*, vol. i. p. 131. Although the birds pair so early, they do not commence laying till the middle or end of May, or even much later in elevated districts. The female lays from ten to twenty eggs, which are of a uniform pale wood, or olive brown colour, and measure in length about one inch and a half, by one inch and one line in breadth.

The hen alone sits on the eggs, and incubation is completed in twenty-one days. The young run immediately that they are hatched, sometimes even with the shell adhering to them. Although the cock bird takes no part in actual incubation, he remains in the neighbourhood of the nest, and will practise all his arts to entice from it any one whose presence may threaten it with danger. As soon as the young birds are hatched, he joins the hen in leading about and protecting them, and the two will, if occasion require, fight stoutly in their defence. Of this Mr. Selby gives a striking instance:—"A person engaged in a field not far from my residence had his attention arrested by some objects on the ground, which, upon approaching, he found to be two Partridges, male and female, engaged in battle with a Carrion Crow; so successful, and so absorbed were they in the issue of the contest, that they actually held the Crow till he was seized and taken from them by the spectator of the scene. Upon search, the young birds (very lately hatched) were found concealed among the grass. It would appear, therefore, that the Crow, a mortal enemy to all kinds of young game, in attempting to carry off one of these, had been attacked by the parent birds, and with the foregoing singular success."

A touching account of the devotion of the Partridge to its young is recorded by Macgillivray. He says: "So great is the affection of the Partridge for its young, that in the very cold and wet summer of 1836, as I have been informed by my friend, Mr. Weir, of Boghead, several pairs were found dead in the fields near Bathgate, with their broods under their wings; they having perished under the influence of cold and hunger rather than expose their tender charge to the inclemency of the weather." In this case we cannot but regret that their affectionate solicitude for their young did not receive the reward it so well deserved.

The young birds continue with the parents until the pairing season, constituting what are called coveys. These vary in number, not only with the number of eggs, but also, as we have before stated, occasionally by two or even three broods becoming united, and following one pair of old birds; in such a case they will sometimes number twenty-five or more. Occasionally a large number of eggs will occur in one nest; even as many as thirty-three are mentioned as having been found under one bird; but there can be no doubt that this number was the result of two hens laying in the same nest, which would seem to be no very rare occurrence where Partridges are abundant.

Hatching is usually completed by the middle or end of June; but this must vary considerably in different districts, and be much affected by an early or late spring. A dry summer is very favourable to the breeding of Partridges, and a wet one equally destructive, the young birds being very sensible to the effects of wet and cold.

Eggs which have been mowed out, or otherwise procured, are readily hatched by the domestic Hen; the young birds should be supplied with ants' eggs, insects, milk, curd, and grits.

The Partridge will, should she be discovered upon her nest, carefully cover the eggs on every occasion of her leaving the nest afterwards: we are not sure if this is invariably the case under ordinary circumstances. Mr. St. John states that it covers its nest and eggs with great cunning: entirely concealing, not only the nest itself, but so disposing the surrounding grass that no vestiges of its track to and fro can be seen. And Mr. Briggs, writing on this point, in the *Zoologist*, says: "I surprised a female on her nest, and she had laid only four eggs; being aware that she was discovered, she covered them very carefully over with dead hedge leaves and dried bents, uncovering them every morning to deposit an additional egg, and then concealing them again. So artfully were they hidden from observation that an eye inexperienced in such matters could not possibly have ascertained the situation of the nest."

The Partridge usually lays but one set of eggs in the year; but should the first lot be destroyed, she not unfrequently lays again. The young birds of the second broods are, however, small and delicate, and seldom survive the winter.

Varieties of the Partridge are not uncommon. Several instances are recorded of white birds, sometimes even whole coveys. These varieties were not produced by change of the colour of the feathers from cold, but were naturally so, being albinos, with red irides. Others have occurred of a cream-colour, with darker markings.

One variety which is permanent in the Vosges mountains, France, occasionally occurs in single specimens in England; in this the normal grey is absent, the whole plumage being reddish brown. This variety has been supposed to be a distinct species by some authors, and has been named *P. montana*. In others the whole plumage is grey. Mr. Tegetmeier exhibited a specimen of this variation at the Zoological Society, in November 1894; and a variety with a white horse-shoe marking on the breast is becoming common.

This light horse-shoe mark appears to be a permanent variety, though some people have supposed it to be a species distinct from the ordinary Partridge.

In October 1851, Mr. D. Graham, of York, showed me an old female Partridge, which was shot by Mr. W. Garwood, near York, about the middle of September, which had the upper mandible very much elongated, and curved upwards and backwards. The bird was in good condition. Partridges have also occurred with large horny excrescences projecting from the breast, being diseased enlargements of the cuticle.

A similar malformation, which ran through most of the covey, is recorded by Mr. J. Dixon, in *The Naturalist*, vol. iii. page 37. He says that a friend of his, shooting near Sherburn, Yorkshire, once sprung a covey of Partridges, out of which he shot eight young birds, each of which had the bill elongated and recurved. "The old birds escaped, which made it impossible to ascertain whether the singularity was hereditary or not."

The adult male has the bill bluish white; irides, hazel. Behind the eye is a small triangular patch of naked skin, red and papillose. Top of head and back of neck, grey brown. Forehead, eyebrows, cheeks, and throat, pale brownish orange. Back, wing coverts, rump, and upper tail coverts, wood brown, spotted and marked transversely with two shades of chestnut brown. Neck and upper breast, bluish grey, with dark grey zigzag lines closely arranged. Flanks, the same colour, banded with pale chestnut brown. On the lower breast is a large horse-shoe-shaped patch of fine chestnut, margined with yellowish white. The wing coverts and scapulars have the shafts of the feathers of a pale wood brown, edged with black. Quills, greyish black, with numerous pale brown transverse bars. Tail feathers, brownish red. Legs and toes, bluish grey; claws, brown.

The adult female has less of the brownish orange on the forehead, eyebrows, cheeks, and throat. The grey brown feathers of the top of the head are edged with white. The horse-shoe mark on the lower breast is either wanting, or else pale in colour, and not so well marked as in the male.

The distinctions in the plumage of the male and female Partridge have been variously and incorrectly described by almost all previous authors; but Mr. Ogilvie Grant has paid particular attention to the plumage of Partridges, and published at length the result of his investigations in the *Field* of Nov. 21st, 1891. A very careful abstract of his conclusions was made by the Rev. H. A. Macpherson, who writes as follows:—" Mr. Grant finds that the only trustworthy characteristics by which a male Partridge may always be distinguished from a female, except when very young, are the following :—

" 1. In the male, the sides of the neck are brownish grey, or nearly pure slate colour, with fine wavy lines of black; none of the feathers have pale buff stripes down the shaft. In the female these parts are olive brown, and almost all the feathers have a pale buff stripe down the shaft, often somewhat dilated or club-shaped towards the extremity, and finely margined with black.

" 2. In the male, the ground colour of the terminal half of the lesser and medium wing coverts is pale olive brown, with a chestnut patch on one or both webs, and each feather has a narrow pale buff shaft-stripe, and narrow wavy transverse black lines. In the female, the ground colour of these parts is mostly black, shading into buff towards the extremity; each feather has a fairly wide buff shaft-stripe, and is also transversely barred with buff, narrowly edged with black. The buff cross-bars on the wing coverts are of an unmistakable character, and quite sufficient to distinguish the hen at a glance. The Partridge assumes the adult plumage of these parts at the first moult; consequently the distinctions pointed out by Mr. Grant are strongly marked in the majority of birds before the beginning of the shooting-season.

"Mr. Grant's researches go to prove also that the horse-shoe mark on the breast is found in birds of both sexes, although it is more liable to vary in size in the female than in the male. In the great majority of young female birds examined the horse-shoe mark was well developed, although in some it was represented by a few chestnut spots. In the old female birds the contrary obtains. In the great majority of old hens, the chestnut horse-shoe is represented by a small patch of chestnut mixed with white. Sometimes the chestnut entirely disappears, giving place to a pure white horse-shoe."

The male is twelve inches and a half in length; the female, twelve inches.

The culinary merits of the Common Grey Partridge are too well known to need any advocacy. To partake of the flavour in the highest perfection, one or two young birds should be cut up and added to a rump steak pudding, with the addition of a few oysters and mushrooms; in this mode of cooking the aroma is better retained than by any other process, and the result correspondingly excellent.

BIBLIOGRAPHY.

DRESSER's "Birds of Europe," Vol. VII., furnishes the most complete account of the distribution of this species throughout Europe.

"The Partridge" in "Fur and Feather Series" contains a good account of the habits of the bird, by the Rev. H. A. Macpherson, with a full description of the modern methods of shooting, by Mr. A. Stuart Wortley.

YARRELL's "British Birds," 4th edition, by H. Saunders, includes a good account of the Partridge, as do most of the volumes on British birds, both general and local.

BOOTH's "Rough Notes" includes a very full account of this species, admirably written, out of the practical experience of the author.

THE RED-LEGGED PARTRIDGE

FRENCH PARTRIDGE.

Caccabis rufa, ... GREY.

Caccabis, from κακκάβη—A Partridge, in classical Greek. *Rufa*—Red.

Perdrix rouge, French; *Perdiz,* Spanish; *Pernice comune,* Italian.

THE introduction of this bird into England took place in the reign of Charles the Second, who had some pairs turned out in the neighbourhood of Windsor, in the hope that they would become naturalised; this, however, does not appear to have been the case, as they disappeared in the course of a few years. Since that period various noblemen and others have introduced them into their preserves, with more or less success; but it seems to be very questionable whether it is any advantage to encourage them to increase, for wherever they have done so the Common Partridge is found to diminish before this more powerful bird; as a Game Bird, too, it is much inferior to its congener, both on the table and in the field. At present it may be regarded as naturalised in several of the southern and eastern counties of England; but only single specimens, which were apparently migrants, have been killed in Scotland.

In Ireland, Mr. Thompson states that he was informed by Mr. T. W. Warren (Feb. 3rd, 1844) that it had been introduced a few years previously into the county of Galway, by Mr. Gildear, but with what success he did not know. Two were shot near Galway, previous to 1844; and one was shot near Clonmel, on February 4th, 1849.

On the Continent it occurs in various countries, particularly the southern ones—in Bohemia, Austria, and Switzerland; is very abundant in France, North-Western Italy, Spain, and Portugal; Jersey, Guernsey, and Madeira; and in some of the islands of the Mediterranean, as Elba, Corsica, and the Balearic group.

The habits of the Red-legged Partridge differ considerably from those of the common species.   In its haunts it is said to be fond of mountainous districts, where there is an abundant supply of wood; and in this country it prefers rough, heathy grounds to the corn and grass fields so congenial to the habits of its congener.   Unlike our common species, which is essentially a ground bird, the Red-legged Partridge will frequently perch upon trees.   Mr. Daniel, shooting near Colchester, "found a covey of fourteen; they were in a very thick piece of turnips, and for half-an-hour baffled the exertions of a brace of good pointers to make them take wing, and the first which did so immediately perched on the hedge, and was shot in that situation without its being known what bird it was.   A leash more were at length sprung from the turnips, and shot; and two days after, a brace more of them was killed by another person."   At Sudbourn "a gentleman, who was particularly anxious to kill some of these Red Partridges, hunted with a brace of capital pointers for them only.   The instant the dogs stood, the red birds ran, and took wing (notwithstanding all the speed exerted to head them), at such distances as to be out of the range of the shot from any fowling-piece."   On the same ground and day, Mr. Daniel succeeded in shooting two brace and a half, hunting with springing spaniels.   He conjectures that they were unaccustomed to the questing of the spaniels, never having before been attacked in that way, and so crouched till obliged to rise.

Since Daniel's time they have increased very rapidly, and are now very plentiful in many parts of the country.   The Red-legged Partridge is not found in Scotland, and does not thrive in Ireland.

When wounded they will run into any hole, such as a rabbit-burrow. These birds also congregate in large packs, instead of remaining, even for a few months, as coveys. The following particulars, taken from Daniel's "Rural Sports," do not apply to the Red-legged Partridge, which is restricted to the extreme south-western portions of Europe —being absent from Germany, Holland, and all the countries east of a line drawn from Brussels to Venice—but to an allied species, the Greek Partridge (*Caccabis saxatilis*):— "According to Tournefort, they are so tame in the Isle of Scio, that they are driven to seek their food in the fields like so many sheep, and that each family intrusts its Partridges to the common keeper, who brings them back in the evening, and he calls them together with a whistle. Another account states that in the country round Trebizond, a man was seen leading above four thousand Partridges; he marched on the ground, while the Partridges followed him in the air, until he reached a certain camp, three days' journey from Trebizond; when he slept, the birds alighted to repose around him, and he could take as many of their number as he pleased."

In Provence persons are said to have acquired the art of assembling numerous flocks of Partridges, which obey the voice of the conductor with wonderful docility; but the suggestion that they were birds of this species which Willughby notices "that a certain Sussex man had, by his industry, made a covey of Partridges so tame that he drove them before him, upon a wager, out of that county to London, though they were absolutely free, and had their wings grown," is obviously incorrect, as the Red-legged Partridge was not introduced into England at the date of publication.

The Red-legged Partridge is, like our common species, monogamous.

According to Meyer, its call-note sounds like the word 'cockileek,' and is frequently uttered during the spring by the male bird.

The food of this bird is much the same as that of the bird last described, consisting of numerous kinds of insects, such as ants, spiders, grasshoppers, flies, caterpillars of all kinds, small snails, corn, young shoots of grass, clover, &c.

The Red-legged Partridge has afforded a remarkable illustration of the manner in which birds may aid in the dispersion of seeds. On December 3, 1860, an example which had one foot and leg imbedded in a hard lump of earth, outside which two toes only were visible, came under the notice of Mr. H. Stevenson, and was exhibited, described, and figured by Professor Newton (P. Z. S., 1863, p. 127). The latter forwarded the incrusted limb to the late Mr. Darwin, who had, in his "Origin of Species," alluded to the possibility of seeds being contained and transported in similar lumps; and the following are the remarks of that distinguished naturalist:—"I have examined the Partridge's leg; the toes and tarsus were frightfully diseased, enlarged, and indurated. There were no concentric layers in the ball of earth; but I cannot doubt that it had become slowly aggregated, probably the result of some viscid exudations from the wounded foot. It is remarkable, considering that the ball is three years old, that eighty-two plants have come up from it, twelve being *Monocotyledons*, and seventy *Dicotyledons*, consisting of at least five different plants, perhaps many more."

The time of pairing is about the same as that of the Common or Grey Partridge, early in the spring; and at this season they are very pugnacious.

The nest, which consists of a small quantity of dry leaves or grass, is placed on the ground in much the same situations as that of the Common Partridge. The female lays from fifteen to eighteen eggs, which have a reddish yellow white ground, spotted and speckled with reddish brown. They are in length one inch seven lines and a half, by one inch three lines in breadth. The habits and food of the young birds are similar to those of the young of the Common Partridge. The Red-legged Partridge will not breed when in confinement, and indeed is not very tolerant of any attempts to domesticate it.

The cock bird does not assist the hen in incubation, but

deserts the nest till the young birds are half grown, when he joins the hen in her care of them.

The adult male has the bill and naked space about the eye, bright red; the irides, red. The upper parts of the head and the hind neck are reddish brown; the forehead, ash grey. The back, wings, and upper tail coverts, and four middle tail feathers are reddish brown, tinged with grey. A portion of the outer web of all the primaries, except the first, and of seven of the outer secondaries, are ochre yellow. The six lateral tail feathers on each side, brownish red. The throat and cheeks are white, tinged with grey; a band of black from the bill to the eye, and thence down the side of the neck, becoming broader, and meeting its fellow on the fore part, where it expands. Sides and fore part of neck, greyish white, tinged with brown, and spotted with black; this part is margined below with greyish brown, succeeded by a broad band of ash grey. The middle of the breast, abdomen, lower tail coverts, and tibial feathers are light red. The feathers of the sides with a broad band of light red, succeeded by another of ash grey, then two narrow bands, one white, the other black, and a terminal band of red. Legs and feet, bright red; claws, a little dusky. Legs with a blunt spur.

The female is somewhat less, wants the knob on the tarsus, and has the colours as in the male, but a little fainter. The black crescent on the neck is narrower, and the spots of the same colour on the lower part are much smaller (Macgillivray).

The length of the male is fourteen inches; of the female, one inch less.

As a bird for the table it is generally considered much inferior to our native Partridge. The flesh is white, but rather dry.

BIBLIOGRAPHY.

DRESSER's "Birds of Europe" gives a good account of the introduction and distribution of this species, with coloured illustration.

SEEBOHM's "British Birds" also gives a full account of the species.

YARRELL's "British Birds" may be advantageously referred to.

THE BARBARY PARTRIDGE

Caccabis petrosa, ...   GREY.

Caccabis, from κακκάβη—A Partridge, in classical Greek.
Petrosa—Belonging to rocks.

Pernice di Sardegna, Italian ; *El Hedjel*, Moorish.

THIS extremely pretty bird can hardly with propriety be called a British bird; yet as specimens have been obtained in an apparently wild state, it has been admitted into the British list by some naturalists. The two specimens which have occurred in England were both females; they both were procured somewhere about the same time. One was picked up dead in a field at Edmondthorpe, about six miles from Melton Mowbray, in April 1842. Mr. Yarrell states that it was afterwards in the possession of Mr. Robert Widdowson, of Melton Mowbray. The other was shot at Sudbourn, in Suffolk, and is now in the possession of Mr. Thomas Goatley, of Chipping Norton, Oxfordshire. This bird is supposed to have been a descendant of some birds hatched from eggs imported into England by the Marquis of Hertford and Lord Rendlesham, about 1770, by whom the country about Sudbourn was stocked with Red-legged Partridges. It has been thought that some eggs of the Barbary Partridge may have been introduced along with those of the other species. This seems to us to be by no means a satisfactory solution of this bird's occurrence in England; for it is hardly likely that the breed would remain so long as seventy years unnoticed, or that a solitary individual should be the only one to be found surviving, *sola superstes*. We incline to the opinion that both these birds were accidental stragglers into this country, or else the produce of eggs accidentally introduced with others at a much more recent date than 1770.

The natural habitat of this bird, as indicated by its English name, is the northern part of Africa; and is elsewhere only found on the Rock of Gibraltar in Europe, Sardinia and the Canaries, Malta, Calabria, and the mountainous parts of Spain; some parts of France, Germany, Italy, and Greece. It is also found in Asia.

Its habits appear to assimilate more to those of the bird last described than to those of the Common Partridge, and we accordingly find it generally frequenting, in its native haunts, such parts of lonely mountainous districts as are covered with small underwood, and where it can follow its instincts unmolested by man.

The nest is placed on the ground, and the female lays about fifteen eggs, which have a yellowish ground colour, thickly spotted with oil-green spots.

It is mentioned by Yarrell that "the Zoological Society have received skins of this Partridge, sent by Messrs. Dickson and Ross from Fezzan. The note appended was as follows:—"Killed in December 1842. Very common all over the country, frequenting ravines, hills, and all places where they can find cover, and often met with even in our gardens; flies in coveys; a shy bird; used as food by the natives, though its flesh is dry and without flavour. Its heart is so small that it does not exceed that of the Sparrow."

The bill is red; irides, hazel; naked skin round the eyes, red. Top of the head and back of neck, burnt umber, prolonged into a broad gorget of the same colour dotted with white spots, which runs to the bottom of the neck in front. Sides of the face, chin, and throat, light ash-colour; ear coverts, wood brown, joining the gorget. Neck above and below the gorget, light ash-colour; breast, buff; back and rump, greyish brown. Quill feathers, brownish black on inner web; the outer web of the first, grey brown; of the others, yellow brown. Wing coverts, slate-colour, the feathers edged with reddish brown. Side feathers with broad bars of white, black, and red brown. Belly, vent, and under tail coverts, buff. Tail, greyish brown. Legs, feet, and claws, red. The legs have a small blunt spur.

The female is like the male, but with less brilliant colouring, and is without the spur.

The length of the male is thirteen inches. The female is rather smaller.

In its culinary value it closely resembles the ordinary Red-legged species.

BIBLIOGRAPHY.

DRESSER's "Birds of Europe" gives a coloured figure of this species, with a good account of its distribution.

YARRELL's "Birds of Europe" figures an English specimen, but maintains that it was an artificial introduction.

SEEBOHM, in his "Birds of Europe," holds still more strongly to the same view.

THE VIRGINIAN COLIN

VIRGINIAN PARTRIDGE.

Ortyx virginianus, ... LINNÆUS.

Ortyx—A Quail, in classical Greek.   *Virginianus*—Of Virginia.

THIS bird is a native of North America, as its name implies. On numerous occasions thousands have been turned out in this country, with a view to its permanent establishment as a Game Bird, but without permanent success, although there seems to be no doubt that it has on some occasions nested. Montagu states that one was shot near Mansfield, which was in the collection of the late Earl of Derby. A number of these birds were turned out many years ago by Edward John Littleton, Esq., on his estate at Teddesley, in Staffordshire, the probable fate of which is hinted at farther on. The Prince Consort also long ago introduced them near Windsor, but they did not succeed. One was shot near Chelsham Court, Surrey, in October 1845, as recorded by Mr. W. Borrer, Jun., who supposes it may have been one of those turned out by the Prince. Mr. Borrer says, "I had a long conversation with the bailiff (who shot the bird), who informed me that it had been heard, and occasionally seen, during two or three months, but that owing to the difficulty of flushing it, it was not till the middle of October 1845 that he succeeded in shooting it. The bird rose from a broad hedgerow, with underwood and timber (which we in Sussex call a 'shaw'), whilst he was beating with some spaniels for a cock Pheasant which had been marked down there. It flew very straight and very swiftly—something in the manner of the Kingfisher. The note was described to me as consisting of two short, low whistles, followed by one long, loud, and shrill." The Rev. Richard Lubbock informed Mr. Yarrell that a nest, with numerous white eggs, was found at Barton, in Norfolk, which, there is little doubt, was that of this bird; for a bird like a Partridge, but smaller, was seen not far from the spot. Mr. Lubbock also states that Mr. Coke turned out a number of these birds at Holkham, in the same county, but he did not know with what success.

A male and female were shot at Rotherfield, near Tunbridge Wells, "a few days before" the 4th of January 1850, and were seen by Mr. Walter W. Reeves, of that place. The female rose with some Partridges, with which it was apparently feeding. Mr. Reeves could not ascertain that any had been turned out in that district. The record is in the *Zoologist* for 1850.

Mr. Yarrell states that a specimen of this bird was shot about fifty years ago in the county of Northumberland, which found its way into the collection of Mr. J. Hancock, of Newcastle-upon-Tyne; "and another was shot off a tree near Bristol, as mentioned by Mr. Hewitson, in the second edition of his work on the eggs of our British Birds. In September 1844 a couple were shot near Egham, as they rose from a pea stubble. On the 29th of October, in the same year, a pair were killed out of a small covey of seven or eight, in a copse near Egham, by Mr. Wyatt Edgell. This latter occurrence was communicated to me by Mr. G. R. Marten, who very kindly allowed me an examination of the birds. And in April of the present year, 1845, a very fine old male bird was obtained, between Weybridge and Chertsey, by a boy, who, hearing the call-note of a bird, whistled a similar note in answer; the bird was deceived by the imitation, and came so close up to him that he killed it with a stone."

The Virginian Colin is found throughout nearly the whole of North America, as far north as Canada and Nova

Scotia. In the middle and Southern States it is stationary, but in Canada and Nova Scotia it is migratory.

The habits of this bird are a good deal like those of the Partridge; but it appears considerably more arboreal, in not only perching readily in trees, but sometimes even roosting in them; the borders of woods, too, are among their haunts, though it would appear that the progress of cultivation induces them so far to change their natural habits as to frequent the corn-fields for food and shelter. Their mode of sleeping or jugging is similar to that of the Common Partridge—in a small circle, with their heads outwards.

They are said to be very pugnacious, and to assemble in large flocks or packs.

They are monogamous, and incubation is performed by the female alone.

The note of this bird is thus described by Wilson :—"At this time (early in September), the notes of the male are most frequent, clear, and loud. His common call consists of two notes, with sometimes an introductory one, and is similar to the sounds produced by pronouncing the words 'Bob White.' This call may be easily imitated by whistling, so as to deceive the bird itself, and bring it near. While uttering this he is usually perched on a rail of the fence, or on a low limb of an apple tree, where he will sometimes sit, repeating at short intervals, 'Bob White,' for half-an-hour at a time. When a covey are assembled in a thicket, or corner of a field, and about to take wing, they make a low twittering sound, not unlike that of young chickens; and when the covey is dispersed, they are called together again by a loud and frequently-repeated note, peculiarly expressive of tenderness and anxiety.

Their food consists of corn, buckwheat, Indian corn, seeds and berries of various kinds, grass, and a large proportion of insects.

As to the sporting qualities of this bird, Wilson says, "About the beginning of September, the Quails, being now nearly full grown, and associated in flocks, or coveys, of from four or five to thirty, afford considerable sport to the gunner. Like all the rest of the gallinaceous order, it flies with a loud whirring sound, occasioned by the shortness, concavity, and rapid motions of its wings, and the comparative weight of its body. The steadiness of its horizonta flight, however, renders it no difficult mark to the sportsman, particularly when assisted by his sagacious pointer."

The following method is adopted, according to Alexander Wilson, in North America, for the capture of the Virginian Partridge :—" To the ravages of the gun are added others of a more insidious kind; traps are placed on almost every plantation, in such places as they are known to frequent. These are formed of lath or thinly-split sticks, somewhat in the shape of an obtuse cone, laced together with cord, having a small hole at top with a sliding lid, to take out the game by. This is supported by the common figure 4 trigger; and grain is scattered below and leading to the place. By this contrivance, ten or fifteen have sometimes been taken at a time. They are sometimes brought alive to market, and occasionally bought up by sportsmen, who, if the season be very severe, sometimes preserve and feed them till spring, when they are humanely turned out to their native fields again, to be put to death some future time, ' secundum artem.' "

The time of pairing and nesting in this country is about the same as that of the Partridge; the nest is, however, very different, being covered at the top, and having a hole at the side for ingress and egress; it is placed on the ground.

The eggs are about twelve in number; Wilson says fifteen to twenty-four, and are pure white. They measure in length one inch and two and a half lines, by one inch in breadth, tapering much towards the small end.

With respect to the time occupied by incubation, Wilson says, " It has been stated to me, by various persons, at four weeks, when the eggs were placed under the domestic Hen. The young leave the nest as soon as they are freed from the shell, and are conducted about in search of food by the female; are guided by her voice, which at that time resembles the twittering of young chickens; and sheltered by her wings, in the same manner as those of the domestic fowl, but with all that secrecy and precaution for their safety which their helplessness and greater danger require." The habits of this bird when surprised with her young are very similar to those of our own Partridge: feigning a broken wing or injured leg, so as to draw attention to herself till the chicks have had time to secrete themselves, which they instantly do when alarmed.

The following account of an attempt to naturalise this pretty little bird in Staffordshire, recorded in *Loudon's Magazine* in 1831, contains many interesting particulars. The writer signs himself J. C. :—"A few years ago I purchased two brace of these elegant little birds from Mr. Cross, of Exeter Change, London, and brought them home with me in the coach. I have a small garden walled round and covered with wire, into which I turned them, but each brace separated from the other by a wire partition. Towards the latter end of May I perceived one of the cock birds carrying straws, and twisting them about over his head; and I found they were making a nest within a bundle of pea-sticks, which were placed in the garden for them to run under and hide themselves. This nest was the joint production of male and female; it was placed on the ground, within the pea-sticks, and shaped much like that of the Wren, with a hole on one side, and covered over at top. After the hen had laid about twelve eggs, she began to sit, and with as much assiduity as our common Hen. When I thought it was her time to hatch, I examined the nest, and found it deserted, and the egg-shells, which had evidently contained young birds, lying about. Much pleased with this circumstance, I went cautiously about to find the dam with her little ones, and after searching a considerable time, the first intimation I had of her presence was from her flying in my face with great agitation, like our common

Hen. I retired much gratified, and observed the young ones, nine in number, collect again under the wings of their mother. The assiduity of this excellent parent was truly exemplary, and her attention unremitting, and she reared them every one with very little trouble. What is very singular, there were eight cocks and but one hen, all of whom were reared till they moulted and got their adult plumage; when, from some cause which I could never ascertain, they began to droop one after another, and before Christmas all the young birds died. Though I examined the stomachs and gizzards of most of them, yet I never could find out the cause of their deaths; but I have little doubt of its being some deleterious substance picked up in the place where I separated them from the old ones, soon after they became full fledged, as the old ones escaped this mortality, and the cock bird is now living (October 1830).

"The other pair never bred, but it was easily accounted for, as the hen was unwell from the first time I turned them down, and she lingered on to October, and then died. Previously to and during the time the hen was sitting, the cock serenaded her with his harsh and singular notes, some of them very similar to the mewing of a cat. He had also a peculiarity of constantly running round in a circle, till the ground whereon he performed his evolutions was worn as bare as a road, and the turf trodden down much in the same way as it is by the Ruff in the fens, during the season of incubation. Nothing could be more cordial and harmonious than this happy family. When the shades of evening approached, they crowded together in a circle on the ground, and prepared for the slumbers of the night by placing their tails all together, with their pretty mottled chins facing to the front in a watchful round-robin. When food was thrown in to them, which consisted chiefly of spirted barley and wheat, and occasionally bread, the male bird would peck at the grain, but not eat any himself until he had called his family around him first to partake of the food; which he did with many soft blandishments, and with much strutting, and spreading of the wings and tail.

"I was much disappointed at the loss of this interesting family, and I waited with some impatience for the result of another season.   The season at length arrived; they built their nest again as usual; the hen laid about sixteen eggs; when, to my great mortification, just as she had begun to sit, I found her dead one morning, and cannot otherwise account for the circumstance than by supposing that something must have frightened her in the night, and caused her to fly up with violence against the wires, which proved fatal to her.   Thus ended my hopes of domesticating this elegant little bird, as I have never been able to procure another female, though I have applied in London for that purpose. The guard of a coach informed me that he had had the care of a basket of these birds by his coach; that they all, by some accident, got out and flew away; and that in the part of country where they made their escape (which I have now forgotten) they had bred and increased exceedingly.   I have also heard of their doing well in some parts of the south of this kingdom.   I know that a quantity were turned down upon the large demesne of Mr. E. J. Littleton, at Teddesley, in Staffordshire, and that they did not breed at all, but straggled away, and some of them were shot ten or fifteen miles from his estate."

The adult male has the bill black; irides, dusky; forehead, black; a black band over each eye; between this and the eye is a white band, extending from the bill, over the ear coverts, half way down the neck; chin and neck, white; a black streak commences at the base of the upper mandible, and running under the eye, swells at its posterior part into a broader band, which, running down the neck, curves forwards and joins its fellow on the opposite side. Upper back and sides of neck, red brown; most of the feathers on the upper parts are edged with blue grey or brownish yellow; lower back, rump, and upper tail coverts, greyish brown, mottled with black; breast and abdomen, yellowish white, the feathers edged with black. Quills, greyish brown; sides and flanks, buff white, marked with chestnut; tail feathers, twelve, bluish ash-colour. Legs and toes, reddish brown; claws, dusky.

The female has the parts of the head and neck which are white in the male, of a light yellow brown. The edges of the scapulars and tertials are whiter than in the male. The upper parts are all lighter coloured, and the under parts have less of the chestnut colour on them.

The length of the male is about nine inches and a half. The female measures half an inch less.

As an article of food, Wilson says, "The flesh of this bird is peculiarly white, tender, and delicate, unequalled in these qualities by that of any other of its genus in the United States," where it is much appreciated.

Audubon says that towards autumn when the young are nearly full-grown they are fat, tender, and juicy, and consequently in great request; but Mr. Tegetmeier, who has partaken of birds bred wild in England, says that their white flesh, though good, is not equal in flavour to that of the Grey Partridge.

BIBLIOGRAPHY.

The full account of this bird must be sought for in works on the American Fauna, such as Audubon's "Ornithological Biography."

MACGILLIVRAY's "British Birds" contains a short account of the species, as do the earlier editions of Yarrell; but its description has been omitted from all recent works on British ornithology.

THE QUAIL

Coturnix communis, ... BONNATERRE.

Coturnix—A Quail, in classical Latin. *Communis*—Common.

Caille, French; *Codornis,* Portuguese; *Codorniz,* Spanish; *Quaglia,* Italian; *Summiena,* Maltese; *Mell'houa,* Arabic; *Soumēna,* Moorish; *Wachtel, Schlag-Wachtel,* German; *Kwartel,* Dutch; *Vagtel,* Danish and Norwegian; *Vaktel,* Swedish; *Peltopyy,* Finnish; *Pérépell,* Russian.

THIS pretty little bird has been well known from the very earliest times, and has excited much attention, from its migratory habits. It is regarded to be the Quail mentioned in the Holy Scriptures as having supplied food for the Israelites in the wilderness; and although this is disputed by some, may be considered as definitely proved by the evidence of Canon Tristram and other naturalists acquainted with the species in its eastern localities.

The multitudes that arrive in the spring, on their way northwards, at all the shores of the Mediterranean, and islands of the Grecian Archipelago, afford a most profitable and valuable harvest to the inhabitants; who, on their advent, sally out and attack them in every way, so that vast numbers must be annually destroyed on the various islands and places where they first alight. Guns, nets, sticks, and stones are all called into requisition, and the whole country is in a state of excitement; and, as Macgillivray says, "According to an eyewitness, enviable is the lot of the idle apprentice who, with a borrowed old musket or pistol, no matter how unsafe, has gained possession of the farthest accessible rock, where there

is but room for himself and his dog, which he has fed with bread only all the year round for these delightful days, and which sits in as happy expectation as himself for the arrival of the Quails." Tens of thousands are often taken in a single day, and yet each year the ranks of this invading yet welcome army are constantly renewed, to be again the unresisting victims of an indiscriminate slaughter. In the autumn they revisit the northern shores of the Mediterranean, on their way to the more southern winter quarters, and are again destined to active persecution by their unsatisfied admirers.

This species of Quail is usually a summer visitant to England, Scotland, and Ireland; but so many are found to remain all the year, particularly in Ireland, that these can hardly be said to be merely accidental exceptions.

On this point we may refer our readers to a paper by the Rev. W. Waldo Cooper, in *The Naturalist* for December 1853, in which he enumerates a number of instances in which the Quail was met with in the winter months; and in the May number for the same year the Rev. Frederic Fane says: "I have thought it singular, that, with one exception, the only occasions on which I have had opportunities of killing Quails, birds supposed to leave England for the winter months, have been in the months of December and January, in Lincolnshire, Hampshire, and Dorsetshire." Mr. Thompson has also collected a great number of instances in which this bird has occurred in Ireland in the winter months, satisfactorily proving to our mind, that a large number, at any rate, do not migrate, and in some districts very few, if any. He says that the climate of Ireland is so mild that the Quails have no difficulty in procuring food during the winter in most years. May not the readiness with which they obtain sustenance materially influence their movements as to migration? He concludes with the following remarks:—
"Although more Quails appear to have wintered in Ireland, in the comparatively mild seasons of late years, than formerly, I have the testimony of a veteran sportsman to the effect, that, from his having met with them in the counties of Down

and Antrim every winter during the last sixty-five years, he had always looked upon them as indigenous, and not as migratory birds. Others bear witness to the same effect for half that period, and have considered them (in the Island Magee, &c.) to be as common in winter as in summer."

Mr. H. Seebohm, in his "British Birds," published in 1885, states that Mr. Lloyd Patterson informs him that the Quail is gradually becoming extinct in Ireland.

However, it is certain that the great bulk arrive early in May, the males coming before the females, and leave in September or early in October. In England and Scotland they cannot be said to be anywhere numerous, while in Ireland they are stated to be very common; and we certainly remember, when living in Dublin a great many years ago, very often meeting with these birds in our excursions into the country, within a few miles of that city. The Quail is generally distributed over Europe, Asia, and Africa. In all these countries they are more or less migratory, and the want of food, rather than change of climate, would seem to be the inciting cause of this movement. Their migration is made during moonlight nights, resting, if possible, during the day. Of course when passing over the sea, their flight must be continued both day and night.

The localities chosen by the Quail in these countries are the same as those frequented by the Grey Partridge—namely, meadows, corn, turnip, pea, and bean fields. It is seldom found on high ground, or in wet, marshy land. The Quail is a ground bird, and it obtains its food in the same situations and way as the Partridge does. The feeding times of the Quail are early in the morning, and again late in the evening till dusk. In the daytime it skulks and hides in fields affording suitable cover, and if the sun be shining warmly, it will bask and sun itself on the sides of hedges, dusting and preening its feathers like the Partridge. Except during their migrations, they would seem not to be of very sociable habits, for the pugnacious feelings of the males are instantly called up whenever two

of that sex happen to meet. The Quail is very swift of
foot, and also flies with great ease and quickness, much
after the manner of the Partridge; its flight is seldom to
any distance, and when it drops it has the habit of running its head into a tuft of grass, or behind any shelter,
imagining that it is then safe, and when in this position,
may occasionally be captured by the hand.

In *The Naturalist* for December 1852 are some
curious observations by Mr. J. M'Intosh, on the hour at
which various birds wake in the morning, from May to
July. He there states that the Common Quail "opens its
eyes to light and life" from half-past two to three.

The Quail is often considered to be polygamous in its
habits; yet this would appear to be doubtful, for in these
countries they certainly seem to pair, and though the male
bird does not assist in incubation, yet he joins the female
when the young are hatched, and aids her in bringing them
up. Mr. Thompson has perhaps collected more evidence in
favour of its being monogamous than any one else, and we
shall therefore make a few extracts from his interesting and
valuable work, bearing upon this point. "The Quail is
generally characterised as a polygamous bird, which I cannot
consider correct, at least in reference to Ireland. The uni-
versal impression, as far as I have questioned persons well
acquainted with the bird, is that it regularly pairs. Indeed
in the north it is generally met with in pairs, not only in
summer, but in winter. Mr. Pool, considering the pairing as
a matter of course, from these birds having so occurred to
him in the county of Wexford, remarks, under date April
11: 'A Quail which has through the winter frequented a
meadow in my daily walk, has, I observe to-day, procured
for itself a mate, but whether from the spring migration, or
from some neighbouring locality, as is more probable, must
remain a mystery, except to the respective parties.' But the
nearest approximation to proof is in the following cases.
The observant gamekeeper at Glengariff (Cork) states that
in almost every instance in which he has found the young

brood, the *two* old birds were with them. My friend Mr. William Ogilby furnishes this interesting note:—'In walking through a grass-field on my farm at Liscleen (Tyrone), about the 15th or 16th of May 1849, I suddenly flushed a Quail, which rose so close to my feet that I was very nearly trampling on it. On looking down, I readily distinguished the lair in which it had been sitting, with a small heap of droppings on one side, evidently indicative that the place had been occupied for some days. But my curiosity was excited by perceiving close by (within about a foot) a dead Quail, which, I presume, must have been its mate, and which, from its condition, I should judge to have lain there for four or five days; during all which time it was apparent that the widowed survivor had never deserted the body. This instance of fidelity in a class of birds of the mental character of which we know so little, strongly attracted my attention, and, I think, may possibly be interesting to you in more respects than one. You will draw your own conclusion as to the value of the anecdote in its bearing on the question of the monogamous or polygamous habits of the Quail. The crop of the dead bird was distended with seeds of grass, mixed with a large number of *Scarabæi* and other insects.' These facts certainly go a long way to prove that these birds are monogamous, in these countries at any rate, whatever they may be on the Continent."

The note of the Quail has been variously expressed by different observers; Mr. Thompson compares it to the words 'wet-my-foot;' Meyer says that in the spring of the year they say 'bubewee or brubrub;' when frightened they chirp like young chickens; and if caged during the time of migration, they incessantly repeat the word 'pievoi-ree, pievoi-ree,' in a fretful tone, at the same time endeavouring to escape. It has also been compared to 'whit, whit, wheet,' 'pickerwick' or 'peekweet-weet.' We have always thought the endeavouring to express the notes of birds by syllables a very unsatisfactory method; there are, to be sure, some exceptions, such as the Kittiwake and the Peewit, where the note is admirably expressed by the name; but let any one attempt to realise, in the fields, half the strange sounds attributed to birds on paper, and he will soon be disgusted with this method of becoming acquainted with the birds, and will seek some other and more satisfactory plan. We make these remarks without in any way attempting to solve the difficulty; we feel it far too strongly to hope that we should ever be able to surmount what has been so unsatisfactorily attempted by others far better qualified than we can pretend to be for this particular duty.

The food of the Quail, like that of other gallinaceous birds, is varied. Mr. Thompson examined the crops of about thirty Quails shot during winter and early spring, and found that seven-eighths of the contents consisted of the seeds of various weeds, among which were those of the various species of Plantain (*Plantago*), Persicaria Dock (*Rumex*), Vetches (*Vicia*), Chickweeds (*Stellaria*). The crop of one bird contained nothing but the seeds of *Stellaria media*, and there could not have been less than three thousand five hundred of them. Another crop was filled with eleven slugs (*Limax agrestis*). To these may be added grain in small quantities; green food such as blades of grass, and other succulent plants. The seeds of the Reed (*Arundo phragmitis*), of the Rushes (*Juncus*), of the Spreading Halberd-leaved Orache (*Atriplex patula*), together with numerous insects in the summer and autumn months. The gizzard also always contains small stones, which assist in grinding up the food. The above list will amply prove that the Quail does much good to the farmer by destroying noxious weeds and insects.

In sporting parlance, a family of Quails is called a bevy; in putting them up you are said to flush or raise them; when at rest they are said to be piped. In speaking of numbers you say a brace or a brace and a half.

Pairing takes place in the spring; the time will of course be dependent, in some measure, upon whether the birds have wintered here or only arrived in May. The Rev. R. A.

Julian, in *The Naturalist* for January 1852, states that
he was informed by a friend that he had seen a Quail's nest
near Ely, containing many eggs, on the 26th of September
1851; when he found it the old female was on the nest.
This was certainly very late for the nesting of this bird; but
it is possible the explanation may be that the first nest had
been taken or otherwise destroyed, which will sometimes
induce birds to incubate a second time.

The nest is simply a slight hollow scraped by the bird
in the earth, with a few dried blades of grass or leaves in it.
Here the eggs are deposited, from ten to twenty in number.
In colour they differ greatly from those of the Partridge—
having the ground reddish yellow, or yellowish white, or
greenish, marked all over with spots and blotches of umber
brown. In length they measure one inch and one line; in
breadth, eleven lines. The time of incubation is said to be
eighteen days, and is generally completed by the middle or
third week in July. The young run as soon as they are out
of the shell, and their food is the same as that of young
Partridges.

We have never heard of Quails breeding in confinement,
but they are readily tamed, and are kept caged in Holland
and Germany as song birds, their plaintive, monotonous note
being much admired in those countries. Meyer says that
a person had a "Quail which had the liberty of running
about his study; and in the same room a favourite setter
dog was allowed entrance: by degrees the two animals
became acquainted, and the Quail might frequently be seen
to lie on the rug near the dog, enjoying with him the
warmth of the fire."

The adult male has the bill a grey brown above, and
a grey blue below; irides, hazel. From the forehead to
the nape is a narrow streak of yellowish white, having on
each side a broader streak of dark brown; over the eye is
another yellow white line, as long as that on the crown.
Chin and throat, white, with a double semi-circular band of
dark brown running down from under and behind the eye,

and having a black patch at the bottom in front. Breast, brown ochre, the shafts of the feathers nearly white; lower breast, abdomen, and under tail coverts, of a yellowish white. The upper parts are brown, with the shafts pale brown. Quills, brown, the outer webs marked with light brown, except the first, which has the outer edge whitish. Tail, of twelve feathers, brown; hid by the upper coverts. Legs and feet, yellowish brown,

The female is without the semi-circular dark marks on the neck.

The young birds resemble the female, and the males are two years old before they attain the dark bands on the neck.

The weight is about three ounces and a half.

The length of the male is eight inches; the female being half an inch less.

As an article of food, Quails are, and always have been, much esteemed. Large numbers are imported alive by the London poulterers, being fattened for sale on hemp-seed.

BIBLIOGRAPHY.

DRESSER, in "Birds of Europe," gives an exhaustive account of the distribution of this species from Ireland to Japan, and southward to the Cape of Good Hope.

CANON TRISTRAM'S "Natural History of the Bible" contains an admirable article proving the present species to be the Quail of the Bible.

THE ANDALUSIAN HEMIPODE

ANDALUSIAN QUAIL.

Turnix sylvatica, ... DESFONTAINES.

Turnix, shortened from *Coturnix*—Wanting the hind toe.
Sylvatica—Found in woods.

Turnix tachydrome, French; *Toirão do mato,* Portuguese; *Torillo,*
Spanish; *Quaglia tridattila,* Italian; *Semmana,* Arabic; *Zer-
quil,* Moorish.

THREE examples of this bird have been obtained in
England. The first-noted was shot in 1844, in a barley-
field in Oxfordshire, within about three miles of Chipping
Norton, by a gamekeeper, who a few weeks afterwards shot
a second; the first only was preserved, and fell into the hands
of Mr. Goatley. The second specimen was so mutilated by
the shot that it was not thought worthy of preservation.

The Hemipode is a resident in Spain, being abundant,
according to Mr. Howard Saunders, near Algesiras, and not
uncommon near Malaga, but elsewhere probably rare, and
also occurs in Sicily and North Africa.

The Andalusian Hemipode is a bird of solitary habits.
It is said to be fond of being among low underwood and
grass, and is very difficult to flush; and when on the wing, it
merely skims over the surface, and takes a very short flight,
dropping, in fact, as soon as possible. After being once put
up, it is extremely hard to raise a second time. In many of its
habits it would seem to resemble our Land-rail, or Corn-crake
(*Crex pratensis*), running very swiftly, as its form indicates,
being admirably adapted to the tangled localities which it loves

to frequent. It is said not to migrate, nor even to remove from the district in which it was bred.

Its food is reported to consist of small seeds and insects. The stomach of the one shot in Oxfordshire contained "two or three husks of barley, several small seeds, similar to charlock, and some particles of gravel."

The possession of habits such as we have mentioned, must render it a bird of very little interest to the sportsman.

The nest, formed of coarse grass, is placed under the shelter of a thorny thicket, and is seldom to be found. In it four or five eggs are usually deposited; these are buffy white in colour, closely marked with dark brown blotches and spots.

The following description of this bird is from Yarrell:— "The point of the beak is light brown, the base pale wood brown; irides, hazel; top of the head, dark brown, with a lighter brown streak in the middle, passing backwards; the cheeks, brown, speckled with buff; upper surface of the body, dark brown, with numerous narrow transverse bars of chestnut, black, and buffy white. Tail, greyish brown; wing coverts, yellowish brown, varied by a dark spot placed on the centre of a larger spot of pale yellow brown; primaries, greyish brown, with a light-coloured line along the edge of the outer web; chin, whitish; throat, neck in front, and upper part of the breast, pale chestnut; sides and flanks, yellowish white, with a crescent-shaped mark of rich brown occupying the centre of each feather; lower part of the belly, vent, and under tail coverts, buffy white. Legs and toes, pale brown."

As in all the Hemipodes, a remarkable group which differ essentially in structure from the ordinary Game Birds, the female is much larger than the male; her length is about eight inches; that of the male, six inches and three quarters.

We have no information as to the culinary merits of this rare bird.

BIBLIOGRAPHY.

YARRELL'S "British Birds," 4th edition, by Howard Saunders, contains very interesting details respecting the habits, capture, nesting, &c., of this uncommon species.

THE GREAT BUSTARD

Otis tarda, ... LINNÆUS

Otis—A Bustard. *Ous*—An ear, on account of its long ear feathers.
Tarda—A Celtic or Basque word.

Outarde barbue, French; *Grosstrappe,* German; *Abutarda,* Spanish;
Batarda, Portuguese; *Pittarrun,* Maltese; *Trappe, Trapgaas,*
Danish; *Stora Trappen,* Swedish; *Dropha, Doodok,* Russian.

IN the olden time, when modern innovations and modern
farming were unknown, the Great Bustard was a tolerably
abundant bird on all the large open plains and downs in England. Unlike the Partridge, which multiplies as cultivation
increases, the Bustard has gradually faded away as the wild
lands have been enclosed and made useful to man; and these
magnificent birds are not now to be seen ornamenting the
landscape. Railways and model farms are now to be found
where in former times the Bustard was the tenant of the
soil; and although few would perhaps wish to resort again
to those times, with their inconveniences, still all must regret
that this noble bird has been of necessity sacrificed to modern
wants and comforts.

The Great Bustard appears to have been very generally
distributed over the country; thus there are records of its
occurrence in Berkshire, Cambridgeshire, Cornwall, Devonshire, Dorsetshire, Lincolnshire, on Newmarket Heath, in
various parts of Norfolk, on Royston Heath, on Salisbury
Plain, and other parts of Wiltshire; on the South Downs
of Sussex; in Suffolk, and in Yorkshire.

With respect to its occurrence in this country, my

brother, the Rev. F. O. Morris, received the following accounts from Mr. E. H. Hebden, of Scarborough, and Mr. Henry Woodall, of North Dalton :—Mr. Hebden says, " I think, to the best of my recollection, it would be about the year 1811 that I first saw the five large Bustards on Flixton Wold ; that number continued there at least two years, when two of them were shot. The three still continued on the same wold for at least one year, when two of them disappeared, leaving the solitary bird, which, after a length of time, was severely wounded by the gamekeeper of the late Sir William Strickland, and was found some days afterwards in a turnip-field near Hunmanby by the huntsman of the Scarborough Harriers, and secured." Mr. Woodall says of some other Bustards, " All the information I can give you respecting the herd of Bustards is, that in the year 1816 or 1817 the late Mr. James Dowker, of North Dalton, killed a right and left shot, and also a third one in turnips, on the farm now occupied by myself. A nest was also found forsaken, with only one egg, which is to be seen at the Scarborough Museum. One of these birds was presented to George the Fourth, through Dr. Blomburgh."

One was seen on Salisbury Plain by Mr. G. R. Waterhouse, on August 9th, 1849 ; it was very shy.

The following is the record of another, Dr. Plomley, of Maidstone, writing in the *Zoologist :*—" I have been fortunate enough to obtain that almost extinct bird in England, the Great Bustard, which was shot at Lydd, in Romney Marsh, on January 4th, 1850. The man who shot it informs me that he had in his garden a wounded Wild Goose, and that the Bustard (which he supposed to be a Goose also), had been seen several times, by himself and others, steadily flying over his garden, and that on the morning of January 4th, as he was standing at his back door, he saw the bird at a distance flying direct to him ; he immediately stepped into his house, got his gun, and killed the bird as it was passing over his wounded Goose. I believe this to be the only instance of its being killed in Kent ; but from the information I obtained during the many years of my residence in Romney Marsh, I think the Great Bustard was not uncommon formerly in that locality. My specimen is a female, and in beautiful plumage. It measures from the crown of the head to the tip of the tail, two feet six inches and a quarter; across the breast with the wings closed, ten inches and a half; from the extremity of one wing to the other, when expanded, five feet and a half. The crop contained a quantity of vegetable matter, principally sea-kale."

The occurrence of the Great Bustard in Devonshire, some time ago, is thus recorded by Mr. J. Gatcombe, of Plymouth, in *The Naturalist* for February 1852. He says, "On Saturday last I was much interested in examining, at the house of Mr. Drew, Taxidermist, Stonehouse, a fine specimen of the Great Bustard, sent to him, for preservation, by Mr. J. G. Newton, Millaton Bridestow, Devon, with a note stating it was shot on December 31st, 1851. The bird being perfectly fresh, and Mr. Drew having only just completed the operation of skinning it when I called, I had the opportunity of ascertaining the sex, and examining the contents of its stomach. It proved a female, and the stomach contained a large quantity of turnip leaves, mixed with several flat flinty stones about the size of a sixpence. The base of the feathers on the breast and back were of a beautiful rose-colour."

One of the more recent examples shot at Feltham, near London, on January 29, 1871, was exhibited in 'the flesh' at the meeting of the Zoological Society, by Mr. Tegetmeier; and in 1879–80 a considerable migration to this country occurred.

Mr. N. S. Hodson, of Bury St. Edmunds, writing in Loudon's *Magazine of Natural History* in 1833, says, " This bird formerly was frequently seen at Icklingham, in Suffolk ; Brandon Heath, and the open fields of Norfolk ; but has not been observed in the first place for some years. The last seen there was a hen Bustard, sitting on six or seven eggs. She unfortunately was disturbed by a farmer, who secured the bird by throwing a casting net over her; but she pined for a short time and died. Bustards are, however, still occasionally seen in the grounds of the Duke of Grafton, at Easton, and on the heaths between Thetford and Newmarket.

"The method which was usually adopted by a sportsman desirous of shooting this shy bird, was to dress his head with boughs, and to walk by the side of a stalking-horse, decorated in the same manner, until he arrived within gun-shot. I have never heard that the breed has been domesticated. The late Duke of Queensbury had three pinioned on his lawn at Newmarket; and Mr. J. Wastall had one pair a long time in his garden, at Risby, in Suffolk. In a wild state, they live on grain and insects, and, according to Shaw, on rats and field mice. They breed among the corn in summer, and in autumn form coveys or flights of about three or four brace. Their flesh is much esteemed by sportsmen."

In Scotland it seems never to have been abundant, Forfarshire and Morayshire being alone mentioned as having afforded Bustards. In Ireland it has long been extinct.

On the Continent the Bustard occurs in many countries. In Germany and Hungary it is abundant, and is by no means rare in France. It occurs rarely in Holland and Sweden. It is also found in Russia, Spain, Italy, and Greece.

In Asia it is found in Astrachan, Syria, and Tartary.

The situations in which these birds are usually found are open plains or downs, and on extensive fields of grain. It is not found among woods or mountains. It is very shy in its habits, and can with great difficulty be approached, even in countries where it is comparatively abundant, as in Germany and Spain. The Bustard is not, strictly speaking, a migratory bird, but remains in its native district the whole year, unless compelled to move from it by the severity of the weather or the want of food; when induced by such circumstances to change their abode, they are said to do so during the daytime, and consequently on these occasions, from their large and conspicuous size, many are shot or captured by the sportsmen in the districts through which they pass. During the summer-time they generally lie close all day, particularly during the breeding season, hiding in the tall wheat or rye. They pass the night in a body; on such occasions they are very watchful, and are seldom surprised.

The Bustard runs with great swiftness; but if approached, it is very ready in taking to its wings, and flies swiftly and well, frequently for several miles. Selby says that the young birds, when alarmed, squat close to the ground, like young Plovers and Lapwings, and in this position may be taken by the hand. This would certainly seem to militate against the old accounts of the young birds being coursed by greyhounds. The male bird has a curious pouch, commencing under the tongue and running down the neck, capable of holding, according to Montagu, three or four quarts of water. The use of this receptacle appears to be uncertain; it is not always present, and is only found in the adult males during the breeding season.

Meyer says that the scent and hearing of the Bustard are very defective, and that if a person can hide in a ditch, or behind long herbage or brambles, near its haunts, and wait the arrival of a flock, he may readily pick his bird, if he only keeps out of sight. In some interesting notes on the Great Bustard, by Mr. Thomas Southwell, in *The Naturalist* for March 1852, the following unsportsmanlike destruction of nine of these fine birds is thus narrated:—"The Rev. R. Lubbock, in his 'Observations on the Fauna of Norfolk,' says that a keeper, by the name of Turner, at Wretham, about six miles from Thetford, some fifty years ago, in severe weather, used to kill many Bustards by looking for their tracks in the snow, and feeding them for a day or two with cabbages. He next constructed a battery of three large Duck-guns, bearing on the spot where the food lay, and secreting himself before daylight in a hole some one hundred and fifty yards from the guns, by means of a long

string fastened to the triggers, he effected a general discharge on the first favourable opportunity; and in this way
he once obtained nine Bustards at one shot." Mr. Southwell mentions that the last Bustard shot in Norfolk, as far
as he has been able to ascertain, was a female, early in 1838,
which was obtained in a turnip-field at Dersingham near Lynn.

After incubation commences, the males do not associate
with the females. During the autumn and winter they
unite together in flocks of from five to fifteen or twenty;
but in some parts of the Continent where they are plentiful,
from fifty to a hundred or more will sometimes be found
collected in one pack.

In feeding, the bill is chiefly used to detach the food;
the feet being but seldom called into requisition.

The Bustard is said by some to be polygamous, but it
does not appear to be known in what proportion the two
sexes exist. According to Meyer, they pair regularly about
March, severe contests taking place among the males, which
are at this time much less wary than at other seasons. The
male, having left the female during incubation, joins her
and her young ones on its completion, and assists in the
care of them.

The food of the Bustard consists chiefly of vegetable
substances, such as grasses of various kinds, clover, green
corn, cabbages, any other succulent plants; seeds, grain,
and insects, in the summer; occasionally also mice, and
probably reptiles. The young birds are said to feed exclu-
sively upon insects. Stones and other hard substances are
also swallowed. We remember once reading of one in
whose stomach ninety doubloons were found, besides small
stones, all well polished and worn; had this been an every-
day occurrence, the estimation in which they are held by
sportsmen would be readily accounted for; the celebrated
Goose which was said to lay golden eggs, would be quite
thrown in the shade in a country where Bustards were
plentiful.

The nest, or rather the place where the eggs are deposited, is simply a slight hollow or depression in the ground; often in a corn or clover field. Occasionally it would seem that it selected other and very different situations for its nest; thus Daniel states that "In July 1806 two gentle-men's servants observed, near Ringwood Forest, a large Puttock Hawk suddenly pitch from the air, amongst some furze, and not seeing him rise again, were led by curiosity to examine what kind of prey he had caught; and which was a young Bustard, weighing nearly seven pounds."

The eggs, which are but two in number, are of a yellowish brown colour, slightly marked with a darker shade of the same. They measure nearly three inches in length, by two inches and one-sixth in breadth.

In four weeks the eggs are hatched; but it is said to be some time before the young are able to run much. If dis-turbed at this time, the female displays her maternal solicitude by shuffling along the ground as if wounded, so as to allure the intruder from the vicinity of her young, who instantly hide themselves as well as they can, by squatting close to the ground: having decoyed her dupe to a safe distance, she soon uses her wings, and makes off, to return to her brood as soon as all is again safe. During the period of incubation the female loses much of her watchful shyness, and on one occasion, some years back, one actually suffered herself to be taken in a casting-net which a farmer threw over her.

In Spain, Mr. Abel Chapman informs us, the eggs are laid in the last week of April (we found two females already sitting, each on two eggs, on the 26th), and about mid-May the males disappear. To Africa they have gone, the local shooters aver; but this, we know, is not the case, and are far from sure that the missing males are not simply hidden amidst the vast stretches of corn, then near four feet high, pending their moult.

Bustards moult very severely, casting all quill-feathers (as Wild Geese do) almost simultaneously. Hence, at the end of May, they become for a time incapable of flight, and natu-rally, under such conditions, seek the utmost seclusion, perhaps deceiving people into the illusion that they had gone, when they are really simply in hiding, which the rank summer vegetation renders easy enough. After eggs are laid, the males certainly desert their mates entirely, forming themselves into bachelor coteries, and leaving to the female the entire burden of the nursery.

From several accounts it would appear that this magnificent bird is, without much difficulty, domesticated; but we are not aware that it has ever bred in confinement. It is greatly to be desired that some systematic attempts should be made to enlist this valuable bird among our domesticated animals; if not, it must in time become almost, if not quite, extinct in most of the countries where it is now found in plenty; just as it has gradually diminished in England before agricultural improvements, and the destructive fowling-pieces now in such general use.

The adult male has the bill greyish white; irides, hazel. Head and neck, ash-coloured; having a streak of black running over the crown of the head to the nape. A tuft of wiry-fringed feathers springs from the chin, running backwards and downwards. On the front of the neck is a long narrow patch of naked skin, of a bluish grey colour, lying over the throat pouch. The upper parts are of an ochre yellow or pale reddish brown, barred with black. Primaries, black, with white shafts; secondaries, tertials, and bastard wing, white; greater coverts, white. Upper part of the breast, pale red orange; lower breast, abdomen, vent, and under tail coverts, white. Tail feathers, ochre yellow, with white edges and tips, and with one or two black bars; tail, often elevated and spread like a fan. Legs and feet, dusky black.

The female resembles the male, but is destitute of the fringed whiskers, and also wants the throat pouch. The male in winter resembles the female.

The young at a month old, says Mr. Selby, are covered with a buff-coloured down, barred upon the back, wings, and sides, with black.

The weight of the adult male is from twenty-five to thirty pounds; the female is considerably less.

The male measures in length about three feet eight or ten inches; the female, about three feet.

As an article of food the Bustard has always been highly esteemed; but in this country, for many years, it has been so rare that but few have been able to indulge in the luxury of a Bustard. Yarrell mentions a pair, in 1817 or 1818, which were sold in London for twelve guineas. On the Continent it is procured more frequently. The flesh is dark-coloured, and Dresser, speaking from practical experience, denies its excellence.

BIBLIOGRAPHY.

Seebohm's "British Birds" contains a most interesting account, written from the personal experience of the author, of the Bustard in the Wallachian steppes, where it is still abundant.

Stevenson's "Birds of Norfolk" gives full details of its occurrence in the eastern counties.

Chapman's "Wild Spain" includes the most graphic description of the natural history and pursuit of the Great Bustard in that country.

THE LITTLE BUSTARD

Otis tetrax, ... LINNÆUS.

Otis—A Bustard, from *Ous*—an ear, on account of its long ear feathers.
Tetrax—A bird known to the Greeks.

Outarde canepétière, Poule de Carthage, French; *Zwergtrappe, Zwerg-
Trappe, Kleine Trappe,* German; *Avutarda pequeña, Sison,*
Spanish; *Cizão,* Portuguese; *Gallina pratajola,* Italian; *Pitarra,*
Sicilian and Maltese; *Booserat,* Moorish; *Rha' ahd,* Arabic.

THIS very handsome bird, which is a very rare occasional visitor to this country, has generally been obtained in the late autumn and winter months. Although
occurring very rarely, as only about fifty English specimens
have been recorded, it has been obtained in many widely-
separated counties; thus it has occurred in Cambridgeshire,
and in Cornwall, several times. Mr. E. H. Rodd, of Penzance, thus records in the *Zoologist* the occurrence of
two specimens in the latter county:—"A female bird in
excellent condition, of this interesting species, was brought
to me for my inspection about a fortnight since, and which
had been brought in by a farmer from the Land's End
district, with some other birds; its value as a rare British
bird was of course unknown, and it was only accidentally
observed hanging in the lobby of one of our hotels with
other game, and supposed to be 'a sort of mottled pheasant;'
weight, one pound and three - quarters. Previous to its
capture we had a tremendous gale from the south, which, no
doubt, drove the bird from the part of the Continent where
it is known to exist plentifully.—November 22nd, 1853.

"Another specimen of the Little Bustard I observed to-day hanging up in a poulterer's shop in this place (Penzance), and purchased it for half-a-crown. I was told at the time that another had been offered last evening, and four or five killed in the neighbourhood. The wind has been from south-east to south for some days, and the bird has been shot for some days.—December 22nd, 1853."

In Devonshire, four times, the last on November 15th, 1839; in Essex, three times; in Hampshire, once at Heron Court; in Kent, at Chatham, in January 1834; in Norfolk many times; in Northumberland, twice; in Oxfordshire, on Denton Common, in December 1833; in Suffolk; in Warwickshire, two near Birmingham, in October 1839; in Yorkshire, on Sledmere Wold, early in 1839; and again, on the 19th of January 1854, a female was shot by the Rev. M. Blow, of Goodmanham, near Market Weighton, and was mounted by Mr. D. Graham, of York.

In Scotland one only has occurred; it was killed near Montrose, in December 1833.

In Ireland a pair were seen in the county of Wicklow, on the 23rd of August 1833, one of which was shot.

Abroad it is distributed over various countries. In Germany, Sweden, and the North of Europe generally, it is rare. It occurs in Greece, Southern France, Italy, Provence, the southern parts of Russia, Sardinia, Spain, and in Turkey. It is also found in Tartary, and in the north of Africa.

In its habits it would appear to resemble the Great Bustard generally. It frequents open champaign country, and seems to be as independent of water as its congener. It avoids mountains and woods; and shelters itself from observation in fields of grain, turnips, or the like. It flies well and strongly, and with considerable swiftness; and, if disturbed, takes wing readily, skimming over the surface of the ground for a short distance, when it alights; and instead of remaining where it pitches, it instantly runs off in a straight line to a considerable distance with great rapidity, and by this means puzzles its pursuer, who probably expected to flush it again near to where it alighted; a knowledge of this habit is indispensably necessary to ensure success in the pursuit of this bird. In its mode of running and general appearance, it resembles the Great Bustard.

The Little Bustard is said to be polygamous, but this is doubtful.

With respect to the note, Meyer says that of the male bird resembles "the syllable 'proot, proot,' which is more frequently uttered during the night; the nestlings and young chirp like chickens."

The food of the Little Bustard during the winter, when, as before observed, they occur in England, consists of vegetable substances. The stomach of one, killed February 1st, 1823, near Twizell, in Northumberland, and examined by Mr. Selby, contained a quantity of stems of clover and grasses, with numerous seeds of the cow-parsnip (*Heracleum sphondylium*), and of other umbelliferous plants. No stones or gravel were found in the stomach. It is also known to feed upon grain, cabbages, turnips, young corn, and other succulent herbs; also during summer, very largely, if not chiefly, upon insects, worms, caterpillars, ants, and grasshoppers. The stomach of one, killed in January 1823, was found by Mr. Yarrell to contain parts of the leaves of the white turnip, lungwort (*Pulmonaria officinalis*), dandelion (*Leontodon taraxacum*), and a few blades of grass.

No nest is made, but the eggs are deposited in a hollow upon the bare ground, generally under some plant or herb which will sufficiently hide the old bird and eggs from casual observation. The eggs are almost invariably four in number, and are generally of a uniform brown olive colour; but Yarrell states that he has seen them slightly clouded with patches of a darker brown. They measure two inches in length, by one inch and a half in breadth.

The breeding plumage of the adult male is as follows :—
"The beak, brown; the irides, golden yellow; the top of the head, pale chestnut, mottled with black; cheeks, ear coverts,

the front and sides of the neck, bluish grey, bounded inferiorly by a border of black passing to the back of the neck; below this a narrow white ring all round the neck, and below this a broad collar of black, with a gorget of white, and another of black at the bottom of the neck in front. Shoulders, back, scapulars, tertials, and upper tail coverts, pale chestnut brown, streaked irregularly with numerous narrow lines of black; all the wing coverts and the base of the primaries, white; the distal half of the primaries, greyish black; the secondaries, patched with black and white; the base of the tail feathers, white, the ends mottled with black and buffy white, crossed with two narrow bars of black, the extreme tips white. The breast and all the under surface of the body, white; legs, toes, and claws, clay brown.

"The males that are killed in the winter half-year have the feathers of the neck of a pale chestnut, streaked with black, like the same part in the female, which does not change with the season.

"The adult female has the head and neck mottled and streaked with black on a ground of pale chestnut; the chin, white; the neck below, without any appearance of transverse bars at any season. The wing coverts have less white than those of the males; the white feathers on the breast, sides, and flanks, are marked with short transverse bars of black. Females in other respects resemble the males."—Yarrell.

The weight of the male is about one pound fourteen ounces; the female, about the same.

The length of one shot on Berry Down, in the Parish of Lanreath, Cornwall, on September 23rd, 1831, is stated, by Mr. J. Couch, to have been eighteen inches from the bill to the tail, and nineteen inches and a half from the bill to the toes. The expanse of the wings was two feet eleven inches.

As a bird for the table, the Little Bustard is often exposed for sale in the markets in Madrid.

Lord Lilford writes: "The flesh of this bird is of excellent quality, and is frequently served up in Spanish inns under the name of 'Faisan' (Pheasant), to which it has no likeness, either in taste or colour. In the Regency of Tunis, where I met with the Little Bustard in great numbers in November and December, and also in Algeria, it is known to the European inhabitants as 'Poule de Carthage.'"

BIBLIOGRAPHY.

DRESSER'S "Birds of Europe" contains an interesting description of the pursuit of the Little Bustard in the Dobrudscha, by Mr. Hudleston.

Lord LILFORD'S "Birds of the British Islands" includes a graphic description of this species as it exists in Spain.

CHAPMAN and BUCK'S "Wild Spain" furnishes an interesting chapter on the Little Bustard, from the sporting point of view.

THE GREAT PLOVER

NORFOLK PLOVER—STONE CURLEW—THICK-KNEED BUSTARD.

Œdicnemus scolopax . . . . . . **GMELIN.**

Œdicnemus, from *Oideo*—a swelling; and *Kneme*—leg; from the thick-
ness of the tarsus in the young.
Scolopax—A bird mentioned by Aristotle.

Œdicnème criard, French; *Alcaravão*, Portuguese; *Alcaravan*,
Spanish; *Masarico de Montes Tellerita*, Maltese; *El Karuana*,
Moorish; *Triel, Dickfuss, Dickknie*, German; *Griel*, Dutch.

THIS fine bird, which would appear to form a connecting
link between the Bustards and true Plovers, is found
pretty widely distributed over this country. Being a migratory
bird, arriving in this country in the spring, breeding with
us, and again leaving in the autumn, it is not probable that
it will ever become extinct; for its haunts are little calculated
for the plough of the husbandman; and we may therefore
look upon the Great Plover as being little likely to meet
with the fate of the Great Bustard, and many other birds
once common in this country; but it is undoubtedly decreasing
in numbers.

In England it is widely distributed, as will be seen from
the following list of localities. It occurs commonly in
Cambridgeshire; several have been procured in Cornwall,
and it is also said to winter there; in Devonshire it is not
common; in Dorsetshire it occurs frequently—at least we
can speak for the south-western part of the county. Essex,
Hampshire, Kent, also possess it in tolerable numbers; in

Lancashire it is rare; it is not uncommon in Lincolnshire; it is very plentiful in Norfolk, as one of its trivial names implies; Suffolk and Sussex are also well supplied with it; in Worcestershire it sometimes occurs, and is not very uncommon in Yorkshire.

In Ireland it is very rare, having only been recognised about half-a-dozen times. One was shot in the county Clare, in the autumn of 1844; another at Clontarf, near Dublin, on January 27th, 1829. Two were seen on the Iveragh mountains in Kerry, in August 1842; another was shot near Brownstown, in the county of Waterford, in March 1840; and the last was shot near Wexford, on December 4th, 1844.

In Scotland only a single specimen has been recorded.

Out of this country, it occurs in more or less abundance throughout the more temperate and southern parts of Europe; in Asia, as far east as India; and is common in the North of Africa.

The localities frequented by these birds are wide open downs, warrens, or large fallow fields, where it can hardly be surprised. We have found it on the open tops of several of the hills in the neighbourhood of Charmouth, Dorsetshire; on these it breeds regularly every year, and have attempted unsuccessfully to shoot it. We never met with it except during the summer months. We first made its acquaintance —certainly only a distant one—on the top of the hill behind Langmoor, near Charmouth; there it used to frequent a very large rough field, much covered with stones; it invariably kept near the middle of this field, and if any person entered it at any point, it would instantly take wing. We never succeeded in seeing it on the ground; and we certainly considered it the most wary bird we ever tried to have anything to do with.

On one occasion a farmer shot one on the top of a hill about a mile and a half distant from the above-named locality; having picked it up and handled it, he threw it, apparently dead, upon the ground, while he reloaded his gun; before, however, he had time to accomplish this, the bird was off, apparently uninjured, and he never had another chance of getting near it. Whether the bird was feigning death, or merely recovered itself, is uncertain.

The males assist in incubation, as was proved by Mr. J. D. Salmon, and recorded in Loudon's *Magazine of Natural History*. He says: "It is generally supposed that the males take no part in the labour of incubation; this, I suspect, is not the case. Wishing to procure for a friend a few specimens in their breeding plumage, I employed a boy to take them for me. This he did by ensnaring them on the nest; and the result was that all those he caught during the day proved, upon dissection, to be males." These birds feed during the night, and like other birds with similar habits, have very large, beautiful, and prominent eyes.

The Great Plover is generally migratory, yet it is certain that some remain in suitable mild districts throughout the year. In Cornwall, Mr. Rodd has only procured them during the winter; and in Ireland most of those recorded occurred during the autumn or winter months. Mr. Salmon also mentions that near Thetford, in Norfolk, he started one in 1834, as late as the 9th of December. There can be no doubt, however, that the great bulk are merely summer visitors, arriving about the middle of March, and leaving us by October, taking along with them the young broods which they had reared.

It seems to require but little water, like the Bustards; for, on the situations it affects, it can scarcely obtain any, unless from the dew-drops on the scanty herbage. In Dorsetshire we never remember seeing one of these birds anywhere in the valleys below its usual haunts.

Of this bird Mr. Thompson says: "A Great Plover in the garden of the Zoological Society, Regent's Park, London, interested me much during different visits in May 1849, by remaining fixed as a statue so long as I had patience to return its gaze, in whatever attitude it happened to be when my eye first rested on its organ of vision. I tried from the different sides of the aviary, and found its performance the same from all. The earnestly fixed gaze of its large and prominent dark eye had a very singular effect."

The Great Plover is monogamous; with the time of pairing we are unacquainted, but it is probably early, as incubation commences before May.

The note of the Great Plover, which is very peculiar, is a kind of shrill whistle, and has been compared to the noise made by the creaking of a winch-handle, or axle of a wheelbarrow which wanted oiling; this may be considered a fanciful comparison, but there is certainly much similarity between the sounds produced by those engines and the Thick-knee. The note is repeated several times in succession, and has been syllabled by the word 'turrlui, turrlui, turrlui.' The specific name, *crepitans*, which has been given to it by Temminck, was applied to this bird in consequence of its discordant note.

The food of the Thick-knee consists of insects of all kinds, particularly beetles, many of which are to be found during the day under the stones among which these birds live; at night they come out, and fall a prey to the sharp-eyed Plover. They also feed on slugs, worms, and, it is said, small reptiles and animals, such as frogs and field mice.

Incubation commences about the middle of April.

The female makes no nest, but lays her eggs on the bare ground, and usually among stones, which afford an admirable shelter from observation, so closely do these birds, eggs, and young resemble them in colour.

The eggs are two in number, of a "pale clay brown, blotched, spotted, and streaked with ash blue and dark brown." They measure in length two inches and two lines; and in breadth one inch and seven lines. The female takes no precaution to hide her eggs or young, farther than by the careful selection of a suitable place for incubation, where the natural colour of the ground, as just stated, gives them almost complete security.

The adult male has the bill black at the point, the base

greenish yellow; irides, yellow. Top of the head and back of neck, pale yellowish brown, each feather streaked in the centre with umber brown; a light-coloured streak runs under the eye from the upper mandible to the ear coverts; beneath this streak is another of brown. The back and upper tail coverts, the wing coverts and tertials, are reddish ash-colour, each feather having a central longitudinal streak of umber brown. Primaries, purplish black; the two first have a large patch of yellowish white an inch and a half from the tips; secondaries, also purplish black. Chin and upper part of neck, white; lower neck, breast, abdomen, and flanks, yellowish white, the shaft of each feather streaked with umber brown. Vent and under tail coverts, ochreous; the tail has the feathers black at the tips, above which is a bar of white, while the upper halves are yellowish brown, with darker markings. Legs and toes, greenish yellow; claws, black brown.

The female does not differ materially from the male.

The young birds are somewhat lighter-coloured, and the markings are not so decided as in the adult.

The length of the Great Plover is sixteen to seventeen inches.

As an article of diet the Thick-knee is held in moderate estimation.

BIBLIOGRAPHY.

DRESSER's "Birds of Europe," Vol. VII., may be consulted for the distribution of the species.

STEVENSON's "Birds of Norfolk," Vol. II., contains a full account of the Norfolk Plover.

SEEBOHM's "British Birds" includes an interesting account of a recent visit to a nesting-place of the Great Plover in Norfolk.

BOOTH's "Rough Notes" contains a very full description of the habits of the Stone Curlew or Norfolk Plover, with a life-size illustration of the heads of the two sexes during the breeding-season.

THE GOLDEN PLOVER

YELLOW PLOVER.

Charadrius pluvialis, ... Linnæus.

Charadrius, in classical Greek, from χαραδρίος—A furrow or cleft,
    from its frequenting such places.
Pluvialis—Rainy, or denoting rain.

Pluvier doré, French; *Chorlito,* Spanish; *Tarambola,* Portuguese;
    Pluviera, Maltese; *Gold-Regenpfeifer,* German; *de Goud Plevier,*
    Dutch; *Hjeile, Brokfugl,* Danish; *Ljung-pipare,* Swedish; *Brok-*
    fugl Hejlo, Norwegian; *Rjanka Sivka,* Russian.

THIS handsome bird is one of the most generally known
and esteemed of the true Plovers; being a permanent
resident, it becomes extensively known from its frequenting
different districts in winter and in the breeding-season; and
in suitable localities it is abundant, particularly in wild districts where it has ample opportunities for nidification and
procuring food. Plovers are generally distributed over the
country; we have met with them on the wild moorland in
the south-west of Dorset; they occur also in various other
parts of the south of England—in Somersetshire and Oxfordshire, but become more numerous to the north, occurring
in Yorkshire and the neighbouring counties in tolerable
abundance, and are by no means uncommon in the York
market.

Mr. Goatley, of Chipping Norton, states that "these birds
come in considerable flocks, in November or December,
and spend some time during the winter months upon the

higher grounds in the neighbourhood, particularly the fields of Chadlington and Dean, between this town and Charlbury, and leave again early in spring;" and it is mentioned by Mr. Briggs, of Melbourne, in Derbyshire, that he has seen a few in his district in August, September, and February, but that they only stay a few days, being apparently on their migration, and merely remaining to recruit their strength. They are not very shy, and visit the margins of the Trent, "frequenting the shallows, where they may be seen running lightly along the shore, to pick up insects amongst the pebbles, and wading knee-deep in the river, occasionally upturning a stone for the food beneath."

In Scotland and the Hebrides it is extremely abundant. It is also of frequent occurrence in Sutherland and in the Orkneys and Shetland.

In Ireland it is common over the whole country, and breeds in all the retired bogs, according to Mr. Thompson; it is very plentiful in the Dublin market during winter. In some parts of Ireland, and probably elsewhere also, this bird, in its winter plumage, is called by sportsmen the 'Grey Plover.'

It is found in France, Italy, Sardinia, and the South of Europe, only on migration or in the winter; and in Norway, Sweden, Lapland, Iceland, and the Faröe Islands during the summer breeding-season.

A very similar bird is also found inhabiting North America and the Asiatic continent, but this is now proved to be a distinct species from the European bird, the Golden Plover having the axillary feathers (which line the under part of the wing) pure white, while the American bird has them hair brown, and the Grey Plover black.

During the spring and early summer these birds are found in pairs, distributed on high boggy and swampy ground, over the whole of Ireland and Scotland, but in England chiefly in the north. During this season it may be readily approached, and will often be heard uttering its plaintive cry from the top of some little eminence at no great distance from you. At other times, Mr. Thompson remarks that "there is a wild life in its cry, which is quite inspiriting."

> " And in the Plover's shrilly strain,
>   The signal whistle's heard again."
>
> LADY OF THE LAKE, 5, xi.

He also very justly observes that this couplet, which has been appropriated to the Great Plover by Mr. Williamson, as quoted by Yarrell, should be more suitably given to this bird; the Great Plover not occurring in Scotland, while the Golden Plover is abundant and well known.

The note here referred to is a shrill whistle, heard to a remarkably long distance, and which might well startle the lone traveller over its retired haunts; Meyer compares it to the syllable 'tluwee,' "uttered at a high pitch, and considerably loud."

Immediately after the breeding - season, they associate together in small flocks of twenty to forty; and as the autumn advances, they collect in larger flocks, and migrate to the south and to the sea-shores, where they pass the winter. During this season we have, as we before stated, in Dorsetshire, observed them to frequent the extensive peaty commons on the tops of the hills about Charmouth; and in that district we never saw them on the sea-shore. In many suitable localities, however, they visit the shores in large numbers. Mr. Thompson states that they are met with on the shores of Belfast Bay from as early a date as the latter end of August, in flocks of from one hundred and fifty to two hundred birds; and he mentions that on one occasion, in the month of January, a wildfowl shooter killed at one discharge of a swivel-gun no less than one hundred and eight Golden Plovers, besides a number more that were afterwards picked up by other persons.

The following account of their habits is given by Mr. Poole, living in the county of Wexford, as quoted by Mr. Thompson :—" The Golden Plover is an irregular winter visitant to the lowlands, coming only when hard frost compels it to leave its highland haunts.   When undisturbed, these birds always arrange themselves in flight in the form of a triangle; but if frightened, they desert that order, and fly a long way (in single file) without joining again.   In feeding on fallow ground, they prefer the furrows to the tops of the ridges, and thus unconsciously form themselves into rank, resembling an army drawn up in order of battle. They are tame birds, and when unaccompanied by Lapwings, easily approached.   Some birds, shot in the evening, had their stomachs distended with earth-worms, on which and beetles they feed."

These Plovers have a curious habit, when shot at, of throwing themselves suddenly down nearly to the ground; and it is said that if a gunner sees a flock of them high above him, he has only, if he has a double gun, to fire one barrel, which will have the effect of bringing them, very probably, within shot of the remaining barrel.   During the winter they may be not unfrequently found associated with the Common Lapwing.   Mr. St. John remarks how well these birds seem to calculate time; for when in winter they are obtaining their food upon the sea-shore, they are (speaking of Sutherlandshire), when the tide is up, obliged to take to the land; and although their chosen resort is, on these occasions, fully five miles inland, they never fail to make their appearance on the shore as soon as ever it is sufficiently uncovered to admit of their procuring food.

The food of the Golden Plover consists of earth-worms in large numbers, small snails, slugs, beetles, and other insects, together with some vegetable substances.   When they resort to the sea-shore, their food is of course very different; and Mr. Thompson has found their stomachs on these occasions distended with small testaceous mollusca of the genera *Rissoa*, *Littorina*, and *Lacuna*, together with the fry of the common mussel (*Mytilus edulis*).

Early in the spring, but depending in great measure on the state of the weather, they pair, and betake themselves to the wild moors and mountain sides for the important task of nesting. The nest is merely a slight hollow in the ground, with a few dry blades of grass in it. The female lays four eggs usually in the second week in May ; these have a ground colour of pale cinereous olive, blotched and spotted with brownish black. They are very beautiful, and exceedingly large for the size of the bird, measuring in length two inches, by one inch and four lines in breadth. They are more pointed than those of the Lapwing.

They breed but once in the season.

The young, which run as soon as hatched, are prettily marked with yellow and brown. If suddenly frightened from her nest, the female generally runs some distance before taking wing. When she has young she is very adroit in leading intruders from the vicinity of her brood, limping off as with an injured wing or leg, till she thinks her progeny are safe, when she flies off, to return to them when the coast is clear.

Incubation is performed by the female alone, and is completed in seventeen days.

The adult male in the breeding-season has the bill dusky black ; irides, brown ; forehead and a streak above the eyes, pure white. On the nape the feathers are black, with the margins golden yellow, upper parts deep black, the margin of each feather being spotted with golden yellow. Primaries, clove brown, with the shafts white ; tertials, nearly black, with golden margins and tips ; sides of neck, white, with spots of black and yellow. Throat, front of neck, breast, and abdomen, pure black ; axillary feathers, white ; tail feathers, brown, lighter at the edges, with darker markings. Legs and feet, dark grey, or lead-colour.

In the winter the upper parts are of a browner black, with a greater proportion of yellow than in summer ; the under parts lose their black tint, and the cheeks, sides of neck, and breast are ashy brown, with a shade of yellow over them ; throat, belly, and vent, white. In other respects as in summer.

The summer plumage is shown in the left-hand figure in the plate. The winter plumage in the figure to the right, in which the head, throat, and upper part of breast only are shown.

The adult birds of both sexes have their plumage nearly alike at the same season of the year; but young birds, during their first autumn, have the breast much darker in colour than the same part of the old birds in winter, and throughout their first winter may be easily distinguished from the parent birds by the greater proportion of dusky grey on the breast and the belly.

The length is ten and a half to eleven inches. The beak measures one inch.

The Golden Plover is an exceedingly good bird for the table, and is held in very general estimation, bringing a good price in the market.

BIBLIOGRAPHY.

Sir R. PAYNE-GALLWEY, in his "Fowler in Ireland," describes all the different modes of netting, shooting, and otherwise obtaining Plovers of various species for food, and incidentally illustrates many points in their natural history.

THE GREY PLOVER

Squatarola helveticus, ... CUVIER.

Squatarola, Italian, of uncertain origin.
Helveticus, Swiss, from Switzerland, the country whence specimens were
   first received.

Vanneau-Pluvier, French; *Pivieressa,* Italian; *Chorlito,* Spanish;
   Tarambola, Portuguese; *de Goudkievit,* Dutch; *Kibitz-Regenpfeifer,*
   German; *Strand-Brokfugl,* Danish; *Kustpipare,* Swedish; *Rjanka
   Tooles,* Russian.

THIS bird is met with in Great Britain at the seasons
of its migration, namely, May and October, being one
of the latest of the shore birds to arrive on its autumn migration. It is very generally distributed round the shores of
these Islands; though it can nowhere be said to be abundant. On the Continent it is found in the northern parts of
Russia and Siberia; on the shores of the Baltic, in Holland,
France, Italy, and Spain. It is also recorded as occurring in
Java, China, Egypt, and South Africa. In North America
it occurs in many places, breeding within the Arctic circle.

In its habits, as exhibited in this country, the Grey Plover
assimilates much more closely to the little Plovers than to
the Golden Plover. It not only seeks its food entirely on
the sea‑shores, being very rarely found inland, but even
when the tide advances, it will not leave the shore farther
than is necessary to ensure it a comfortable standing-place,
until it can again return to its feeding-ground. In this
country it is never seen in large flocks; two or three, or at
most a dozen or twenty, being the usual number seen: it

157

seldom mixes with birds of other species. It is so extremely watchful and suspicious, that it is only obtainable with great difficulty; and even if tolerably common in any locality, it may be some time before one can be shot. During the night it seems to put on a double amount of wariness, and at that time it is almost impossible to get near it. Flat, sandy, and muddy shores are those most frequented by this bird. Its chief feeding times are early in the morning and late in the evening; but it probably also feeds much during the night, like the other Plovers, and for doing which its large eye would seem specially adapted. In America, during the spring and summer, they frequent fields remote from the sea. Wilson says: "It generally makes its first appearance in Pennsylvania late in April, frequents the countries towards the mountains, seems particularly attached to newly-ploughed fields, where it forms its nest of a few slight materials, as slightly put together. About the beginning of September they descend with their young to the sea-coast, and associate with the numerous multitudes then returning from their breeding-places in the north. At this season they abound on the plains of Long Island."

Its note is a loud whistle; according to Thompson, a double whistle.

The food consists, when inland, of insects of all kinds, worms, and various berries, particularly those of the *Vaccinia*, and allied species. When feeding on the shores, as in this country, it lives on marine insects, small crustacea, various small marine mollusca, sea-worms, and a small quantity of some sea-weeds.

Its nest, according to Wilson, is placed on the ground, often in newly-ploughed fields, and is very simple in its structure and materials.

It lays four eggs, having a ground colour of light olive, dashed with black. They are large for the size of the bird. European specimens were formerly great desiderata, but were obtained from the banks of the Petchora, in 1875, by Messrs. Seebohm and Harvie Brown.

The adult male in summer has the bill black; forehead and streak over the eyes, white. Between the bill and the eye, the ear coverts, sides of the neck, breast, and belly, black; thighs, vent, and under tail coverts, white. Feathers of top of head and nape, hair brown, with lighter edges; back and scapulars, black, or deep brown, nearly black, each feather edged with white. Primaries, brownish black, with white shafts; axillary feathers, black; tail coverts, white, with brown bars; tail, of twelve feathers, white, with blackish bars. Legs and feet, dark lead-colour.

In the winter the forehead is white; the top of the head and upper parts are hair brown, each feather having its margin spotted with grey and yellowish spots; upper tail coverts, white; tail, white, with brown bars; chin and throat, white; neck and ear coverts, white, with a brown streak on each shaft; breast and upper part of belly and flanks, white, spotted with hair brown; belly, thighs, and vent, white. The female is like the male.

Young birds of the year in autumn are much spotted with yellow, and resemble the Golden Plover, from which they are readily distinguished by their axillary feathers being black, and the possession of a small hind-toe.

Weight, about seven ounces.

The length is twelve inches. Expanse of wings, two feet.

As an article of food the Grey Plover is generally considered to be much inferior to the Golden Plover, and may be purchased in the market for a considerably smaller sum.

BIBLIOGRAPHY.

SEEBOHM, in "Siberia in Europe," describes the nesting of this species in the marshes of the Petchora river. The account is reproduced, with additions, in the "British Birds" of the same author.

THE DOTTEREL

DOTTEREL PLOVER.

Eudromias morinellus, ... LINNÆUS.

Eudromias, from ενδρομίας—A good runner.
Morinellus, diminutive from *Morus*—A simpleton.

Pluvier guignard, French; *Dummer Regenpfeifer*, German; *Piviere tor-
tolino*, Italian; *Morinel Plevier*, Dutch; *Pomerantzfugl*, Danish;
Fjällpipare, Swedish; *Pomerantsfugl*, Norwegian; *Keräjäkur-
mitsa*, Finnish; *Zuck glupöi*, Russian.

THE Dotterel, coming to this country merely for the
purpose of incubation, is only seen during the spring
and summer months, leaving us again in the autumn; it
breeds in Scotland and the extreme north of England, and
possibly in Ireland, and can only be looked upon as a passing visitor in the more southern counties. It was formerly
plentiful in the eastern counties, but has now become very
rare, not being found in the districts where it previously was
common. Dresser says that unless the Bird Protection Act
interferes, it will soon be an unknown bird amongst us. It
formerly passed, in spring and autumn, through Berkshire,
Cambridgeshire, Hertfordshire, Norfolk, Suffolk, and Wiltshire, in small flocks; while in Dorsetshire, Devon, and
Cornwall, it occurred rarely. It was, however, reported to
breed occasionally on the high range of the Mendip Hills, in
Somersetshire. Passing on to the north, it occurred in the
shires of Lincoln, Derby, and York; and in Lancashire,
Westmoreland, and Cumberland. In Scotland it was only a

passing visitor in the Lowlands, but bred on many of the lofty hills in that country. Mr. C. St. John, speaking of Sutherlandshire, says it is rare, but that it breeds on Clee-brick; he also mentions the singular fact, that although on any given hill you may find thousands of the Golden Plover breeding, you will only find one pair of Dotterels. In Ireland the Dotterel is very rarely met with. Mr. Thompson records several instances of its occurrence, only one of which was during its spring migration; one, however, occurred near Clonmell, on Sliev-na-mon mountain, on the 24th of June 1835, and was shot by Mr. R. Davis, Jun., of Clonmell, in company with Golden Plovers. The others occurred in August or September.

Having succeeded in rearing their young, they pass to the southward during the month of September, and are again seen in most of the places which they visited in the spring, before they finally leave our shores for their winter retreat in North Africa. Yarrell says that some few winter in the south of Italy, Sicily, and the Levant. They breed in all the northern countries of Europe; in France they are only passing visitors, going to the north in the spring, and returning south in the autumn.

The habits of the Dotterel lead them to select the higher parts of the most lofty mountains for the purpose of incubation; and Mr. St. John says that only a single pair will be found breeding on each hill. Mr. Heysham, of Carlisle, states that they chiefly select those hills that are covered with the woolly fringe moss (*Trichostomum lanuginosum*, Hedw). This gentleman had good opportunities of studying the habits of these birds, and has written at some length upon them. His observations show that in the neighbourhood of Carlisle they are by no means solitary in their disposition in the breeding-season, but that several pairs associate together in the greatest harmony at these times. They appear to be very careless of the approach of man. Mr. Heysham says: "On the 3rd of July we found three or four pairs near the most elevated part of this mountain (Robinson); and on all our visits thither, whether early in the morning or late in the afternoon, the greater part were always seen near the same place, sitting on the ground. When first discovered, they permitted us to approach within a short distance, without showing any symptoms of alarm; and frequently afterwards, when within a few paces, watching their movements, some would move slowly about and pick up an insect, others would remain motionless, now and then stretching out their wings, and a few would occasionally toy with each other, at the same time uttering a few low notes, which had some resemblance to those of the Common Linnet. In short, they appeared to be so very indifferent with regard to our presence, that at last my assistant could not avoid exclaiming, 'What stupid birds these are!' The female that had young, nevertheless, evinced considerable anxiety for their safety whenever we came near the place where they were concealed; and as long as we remained in the vicinity, constantly flew to and fro above us, uttering her note of alarm." "One, on quitting them (the eggs), immediately spread out its wings and tail, which it trailed on the ground a short distance, and then went away without uttering a single note." Mr. H. says that they vary much in the time of commencing incubation—old females sometimes beginning to lay as early as the 26th of May; while a perfect egg has been taken out of a female, shot on Robinson, as late as July 19th. The middle of June is, however, the most usual time.

The Dotterel is very fond of dusting itself, and will frequently do this even while a spectator is within a few yards of it.

The singular tameness, or stupidity as it has been called, of the Dotterel in the presence of man, and its habit of stretching out a leg or wing, probably led to the old fable that it imitated the actions of any person approaching it; thus it used to be said, that when the fowler raised an arm, it raised a wing; if he elevated a leg, it did the same, and was so intent on watching his actions as to allow him to advance till he was able to secure it in his net.

In former times the Dotterel used to be captured in

nets; Daniel, quoting from Willughby, says : " Six or seven persons go in company; when they have found the birds, they set their net in an advantageous place, and each of them, holding a stone in either hand, get behind the birds, and striking the stones often one against another, rouse them from their natural sluggishness, and by degrees drive them into the net." This practice is, however, now entirely abandoned, at least in this country; the gun affording a much readier and more effective method of destruction.

Dotterels are monogamous. Their food consists of insects, chiefly small beetles, caterpillars, worms, small snails, and grasshoppers.

No nest is made, but the eggs are deposited "in a small cavity on dry ground, and generally near a moderate-sized stone or fragment of rock." The eggs, usually three in number, are yellowish olive colour, blotched and spotted with dark brownish black.

Incubation is believed to continue for eighteen or twenty days; and the males assist the females in their arduous yet pleasing labour.

The Dotterel is readily tamed, but it is said not to live long in confinement.

The adult male, in summer plumage, has the bill black; irides, brown ; top of the head and nape, rich brown. Over the eye, running backwards and downwards, is a band of pure white. Chin and sides of upper neck, white; ear coverts, back of neck, and back, ash-coloured; scapulars, wing coverts, and tertials, greyish brown, edged with pale orange brown. Primaries, hair brown, or ash grey, the shaft of the first, white; front and sides of lower neck, ash-colour; below this is a white gorget, surrounded by a dark line; below this the breast, belly, and sides shade gradually into rich brownish orange, the centre of the belly being black. Vent and under tail coverts, white, tinged with rufous; tail feathers, ashy brown, becoming darker towards the ends, the tips white ; the three outside feathers have large tips of white. Legs and feet, olive; claws, black.

The winter plumage would seem, from specimens obtained early in the spring before the breeding dress was assumed, to have the breast and belly nearly white, and the colour on the head less deep.

In length the Dotterel measures nine inches and a half.

The Dotterel is greatly esteemed by epicures for the delicacy of its flesh, and meets a ready sale whenever it is brought into the market.

BIBLIOGRAPHY.

Mr. Heysham's graphic account of this species, published fifty years ago in the *Magazine of Natural History*, has been reprinted in most works on British birds, and may be taken in conjunction with Captain Fielden's description in Dresser's ' Birds of Europe," as nearly exhausting what is known respecting the Dotterel.

THE RINGED PLOVER

Ægialitis hiaticula, ... Linnæus.

Ægialitis, αἰγιαλῖτις—Of the shore.
Hiaticula—After Aristotle: so called from its haunting the mouths of
rivers.

Pluvier à collier, French; *Lavadeira*, Portuguese; *Frailecillo*, Spanish;
Corriere grosso, Italian; *Monachella prima*, Maltese; *Sand-
Regenpfeifer*, German; *de boutbekkige Plevier*, Dutch; *Stor Strand-
piber*, Danish; *Tukagvajok*, Greenlandic; *Sandtoa*, Icelandic;
Strandryle, Strandvibe, Norwegian; *Större Strandpipare, Sand-
rulling*, Swedish; *Tyllikurmitsa*, Finnish.

EVERY person who has at any time occupied himself in
shore shooting must be familiar with this very pretty
and lively little bird. It is very generally distributed round
all our shores; wherever any sand or shingle is left exposed
by the retiring tide, there will this active little bird be found
foraging for food at the very edge of the water.

Out of this country it occurs all over the shores of
Northern Europe, ranging eastward into Western Asia, and it
winters in Africa as far south as the Cape.

The Ringed Plover is resident with us throughout the
whole year; but as the winter draws on, a large accession to
their numbers is received from the north. The migrations
are performed during the night.

Although their habits are maritime, yet they will not unfrequently ascend some of our rivers for considerable distances, for the purpose of incubation; sometimes as far as
twenty miles from the sea. They also frequent the extensive

warrens of Norfolk and Suffolk for the same purpose.   In seeking its food, the Ringed Plover runs along the margin of the water very quickly, with its head and neck stretched forwards.   It turns sharply to either side, picking up little crustacea and other marine insects.   It flies very quickly. On being disturbed, it will fly a short distance seaward, returning again to the land, and settling probably within a couple of hundred yards of the point from which it started.   It is very fond of associating with the large flocks of Dunlins (*Tringa alpina*) which frequent the same localities; and a Ringed Plover not unfrequently falls to the gun directed among a flock of Dunlins.   They also unite together in flocks, but very frequently may be found in smaller numbers.   In the spring they congregate into large flocks, preparatory to migration.

They are monogamous, and during the time of breeding are found more scattered in single pairs, than at other times.

Their note is pleasing, though monotonous; the call-note has been syllabled by Meyer, by the word 'trull, trull, trull;' and their cry, when alarmed, by the word 'truwee.'

As we have before remarked, it is by no means easy to convey by letters a correct idea of the note of any bird.   It must be heard to enable any one to recognise it.

The food of this little Plover consists of minute crustacea and other marine insects; of small shelled-mollusca, and probably insects of all kinds that come within its ken.   When frequenting the banks of rivers, inland lakes, or ponds, its food probably consists of the minute beetle so common in such situations, and some of the fresh-water mollusca.

Pairing takes place early in the spring.   The nest consists of a slight hollow in the sand or shingle of the beach they frequent.   The bottom of this has sometimes fragments of shells arranged in it, evidently brought by the bird; and rarely the eggs are deposited upon some of the dried sea-weed to be met with in their haunts.   It also nests in the sandy warrens of Norfolk and Suffolk at a considerable distance from the sea.

The eggs are four in number, and are of a cream colour, streaked and spotted with blue and black. They measure one inch and five lines in length, by one inch in breadth.

Incubation is usually completed from the middle to the end of May, and is said to last for fifteen or sixteen days.

During the period of incubation, which is performed by both parents, if they are disturbed, they usually first run from the nest, and then fly off without any cry or noise; if, however, frightened after the young are hatched, they betray usual anxiety, flying round in circles, crying, and trying to call off attention from the young brood; which in the meantime are hiding by squatting among the stones around them. The young birds are able to run soon after quitting the egg.

Varieties of this bird are by no means common. The following is recorded by Mr. Thompson :—" A singular variety of the Ringed Plover was shot on the 1st of August 1842, in Belfast Bay. It is wholly white, except where the plumage is ordinarily blackish, that is, on the gorget, the primaries, and a band towards the extremity of the tail; all of which are, instead, of a very pale yellowish brown. The portions of the plumage usually of a very pale yellowish white cast, are in this bird of a pure white. Bill, pale brown, instead of black; legs, yellowish. The specimen is preserved in the Belfast Museum."

The male has the bill black at the tip, the remainder yellow, shading into orange at the base; irides, brown; lower part of the forehead, cheeks, and ear coverts, black; on the forehead is a band of white, running down to the eye. Crown, black; back of crown and nape, hair brown; over the ear coverts and eye is frequently a pale streak. Chin and collar round the neck, white; below this is a collar of black, broad in front, narrow behind. Back, wing coverts, tertials, and upper tail coverts, uniform hair brown; primaries, blackish brown; part of the shafts near the tips, white; secondaries and greater wing coverts, tipped with white, forming a bar across the wing, visible when the wings are extended. Tail feathers, hair brown at the base, shading nearly into black towards the end; the centre feathers have a slight white tip, becoming wider on the others towards the sides; the outside one is altogether white, and the second has its outside web of that colour. Breast, belly, vent, and under tail coverts, white; legs and toes, orange yellow; claws, black.

The female resembles the male.

In the young birds the bill is dusky; they are without the black band on the forehead; the other dark parts of head and neck are ashy brown. Legs and feet, pale yellow.

The length is about seven inches and three-quarters; but specimens differ so much in size that some ornithologists regard them as distinct; but intermediate sizes occur.

BIBLIOGRAPHY.

STEVENSON's " Birds of Norfolk " contains an interesting account of the breeding of this species in inland warrens, by Professor Newton and his brother.

THE KENTISH PLOVER

Ægialitis cantiana, ... LATHAM.

Cantiana—First sent to Latham from Kent.

Pluvier à collier interrompu, French; *Lavadeira,* Portuguese; *Charran,* Spanish; *Fratino,* Italian; *Bou-hejaira,* Moorish; *See-Regenpfeifer,* German; *Strandplevier,* Dutch; *Hvidbrystet Strandpiber,* Danish; *Hvitbröstad Strandpipare,* Swedish.

THE trivial name of this Plover would give the idea that it was only to be procured in the county of Kent; there, certainly, the first specimens were obtained between sixty and seventy years ago, and on its coast some are still to be found; yet it has since occurred along the shores of Norfolk, Kent, and Sussex, where a few remain to breed, and is probably to be met with on other parts of the coast.

In Scotland it has not been recorded.

In Ireland it has occurred as far north as Belfast, where Mr. Thompson states it has been shot on two occasions, but only one specimen was preserved. It is a summer visitor to England, arriving in May, and leaving in September.

Out of these countries it is found in the temperate and warmer parts of Europe during summer, and winters in Africa, India, and the south of China.

In habits and food it closely resembles the bird last described.

It is to be found in the same situations, mixing with the Ringed Plovers, but, it is said, not flying off with them when disturbed.

The nest is merely a slight hollow in the sand or fine

shingle, on the beach just above high-tide mark; in this four eggs are deposited, the ground colour of which is a yellowish stone, with streaks and spots of black. They measure in length one inch and a quarter, by eleven lines in breadth.

According to Meyer, incubation lasts seventeen days.

The habits of the young, and of the old birds in protecting their progeny, are similar to those of the Common Ringed Plover.

In the adult male the bill is black; irides, brown; the forehead, a streak over each eye, the cheeks, sides of neck and collar round it, breast, belly, vent, and under tail coverts, pure white. Above the white forehead is a band of black; a black streak runs from the bill to the eye; ear coverts black. From the point of each wing a patch of black extends forwards on the breast, but the two do not join in the centre, which is white. Top of head and nape, reddish brown; back and wings, light hair brown; primaries, brownish black, with white shafts; secondaries, tipped with white; centre tail feathers, dusky black, lighter towards the base; the outside two feathers on each side, white. Legs, feet, and claws, black.

In the female the black on the head and neck is rather smaller in quantity, and not so decided in colour.

In the young birds the black patch above the forehead is wanting, and what is black in the adult is of a browner tint in the young bird. The bill, legs, feet, and claws, black.

The length is about seven inches.

In its culinary merits this bird agrees with the other species of the genus.

BIBLIOGRAPHY.

BOOTH's " Rough Notes " gives an account of the gradual diminution of this species on the coast of Norfolk, owing to the pursuit by collectors.

THE LITTLE RINGED PLOVER

Ægialitis curonica, ... **GMELIN.**

Curonica—From *Curonia* (*Courland*), on the Baltic.

Petit Pluvier à collier, French; *Lavadeira,* Portuguese; *Frailecillo,*
Spanish; *Monakella sekonda,* Maltese; *Fluss-Regenpfeifer,* Ger-
man; *Kleine Plevier,* Dutch; *Prostekrave, Sandevit, Tudse, Tijhit,*
Danish; *Liden Strandryle,* Norwegian; *Mindre Strandpipare,*
Swedish; *Pieni ranta raukuja,* Finnish.

THIS bird can only be described as a rare straggler to
the coasts of England, although not uncommon in
Europe, migrating to Africa in the winter. Mr. Gould wrote
in the "Birds of Europe:"—"We are indebted to our friend,
Mr. Henry Doubleday, of Epping, for the loan of an example of this elegant little Plover, which, he informs us, was
taken at Shoreham, in Sussex. From the extreme youth of
the specimen transmitted to us, it is clear that it must have
been bred on the spot; and it is worthy of notice that the
person who killed it affirms that he has long suspected the
present bird to be a resident on that part of the coast, from
having remarked that he could always perceive a difference in
the note of this bird from that of either of the other species.
Whether this Plover habitually resorts to our shores or not,
it may now reasonably claim a place in the Fauna of our
Island." Mr. Yarrell further states that the Rev. R. Lubbock,
in his recently-published "Fauna of Norfolk," says that "two
specimens of this bird in the Norwich Museum were believed
by Mr. Denny, the Curator, to have been killed in the county;
but the fact was not noted down at the time."

It has not been recognised in either Scotland or Ireland.

On the Continent it is not uncommon; but it is not so northern in its range as the Ring Plover; it, however, occurs in Sweden, Holland, Germany, France, and Italy. In Asia it is said to occur in Nepal, about Calcutta, and in Japan.

It migrates from the warmer latitudes to temperate countries for the purpose of incubation; returning again southwards when that is completed.

Its habits seem to be very much like those of the Common Ringed Plover, except that it is more frequently found on the sides of rivers than its congener; appearing to prefer them to the sea-shore. Its food is also similar.

Its nest, which is frequently placed on some of the sandy islands found in the larger continental rivers, is, according to Meyer, "a perfect rounded cavity in the ground, or layer of small stones;" and is generally placed "where the smallest particles of gravel cover the surface of the ground, but never on the fine sand." Yarrell, on the authority of Mr. Hoy, states that "it lays its eggs on the sands; not a particle of grass or other material being used."

The eggs are said to be four in number, of a pale yellowish stone-coloured ground, with numerous small three-coloured spots, namely, "bluish ash, red brown, and dark brown."

The adult bird has "the beak black; the irides brown; the forehead white, with a black patch above it, extending to the eye on each side; top of the head and the occiput, brown; lore and ear coverts, black; nape of the neck, white. Back, scapulars, wing coverts, tertials, rump, and upper tail coverts, ash brown; primary and secondary wing feathers, dusky brown; these and the greater wing coverts edged with white. The first primary quill feather, with a broad white shaft; tail feathers, ash brown at the base, darker towards the end. The five outer tail feathers on each side, white at the end; this colour increasing in extent on each lateral feather, the outer one on each side having only a dusky spot on the inner web, but this appears to be constant at all ages; chin and throat, white—this colour extending from the latter round the nape of the neck; below this and above the breast is a collar of black. The breast itself, the belly, vent, and under tail coverts, pure white; legs and toes, flesh-colour, tinged with yellow; the claws, black.

"Adult females have the white and black frontal bands narrower than the males, according to M. Temminck, and they are also less perfectly defined.

"Young birds of the year want all the decided black markings which distinguish old birds, and the ash brown feathers of the back and wing coverts have buff-coloured margins."—Yarrell.

The length is about six inches and a quarter.

Respecting its culinary merits we have no special information.

BIBLIOGRAPHY.

Dresser's "Birds of Europe" contains a full description of the distribution in Europe and of the habits of this rare straggler to our coasts.

THE WOODCOCK

Scolopax rusticula, ... LINNÆUS.

Scolopax. Skolops—A stake sharpened at one end: from the form of
its bill.
Rusticula—Belonging to the country.

Bécasse, French; *Gallinhola,* Portuguese; *Chocha, Gallineta Becada,
Sorda,* Spanish; *Beccaccia,* Italian; *Gallina,* Maltese; *Himar el
hedjel,* Moorish; *Waldschneppe,* German; *Houtsnip, Woudsnep,*
Dutch; *Skovsneppe,* Danish; *Rugde, Holtsneppe,* Norwegian;
Morkulla, Swedish; *Lehtokurppa,* Finnish; *Bekass-slomka, Sha-
bashka,* Russian.

THE Woodcock, though frequently breeding with us, is,
as far as sporting or gastronomic purposes are con-
cerned, a winter visitor to this country. The flocks or flights
arrive in considerable numbers upon our shores, usually about
the end of September or the beginning of October first;
making their appearance near the line of coast, and after resting a day or two, distributing themselves over the inland
country, in places suited to their habits. With respect to
the east and south coasts of England, this is well ascertained
to be the case; and speaking of the west coast of Ireland,
Mr. Thompson says: "Mr. G. Jackson (gamekeeper to the
Earl of Bantry, at Glengariff) states that on the Woodcocks'
arrival from their northern breeding-places they are always
seen first on the very western shores. He has invariably
found them near Dursey Island some days before they appeared inland. This fact is well known to sportsmen living
on the western coast of Ireland."

It is not easy to account for this curious habit, for it is

generally supposed that most of the Woodcocks which visit
this country are bred in Norway, Sweden, and Lapland; it
seems, therefore, singular that they should not first be found
on the east coast of England and Scotland, and afterwards
spread themselves to the westward, as they would thus be
able to rest themselves after a comparatively short flight over
the German Ocean. The most probable explanation is that
the climate is milder and the frost less severe near the coast,
and the birds seek the warmer temperature, reaching the shore
in their nocturnal flights.

In their autumnal migration the females are the first to
arrive; few, if any, males being found among the first flight
to any particular locality; they are, however, soon followed
by the males.

Like many other migratory birds, the Woodcock chooses
the night for performing its flight, and very generally, if not
always, arrives at its destination by or before daybreak. It
would seem, from the testimony of various people who have
been fortunate enough to witness the arrival of a flight of
Woodcocks, that, migrating as they do at a great height in
the air, they descend almost perpendicularly to the ground
at the termination of their journey.

On the east coast of England, they arrive in good condition, proving that their flight has not been of any long
continuance; on the south - west coast, near Plymouth, we
have the authority of the Rev. R. A. Julian for stating
that they arrive there with the breast-bone prominent and
sharp, as if their migration had extended over a considerable
period of time; but he adds that a very few days is sufficient
to restore them to their usual state of plumpness. Mr. Selby
says that Woodcocks "always come over in the greatest bodies
in hazy weather, with little wind, and that blowing from the
north-east; and it is probable they find the upper region of
the atmosphere, in which they fly, freer from counter-currents
of air than in more open weather. After a night of this description I have frequently met with great numbers upon the
edges of plantations, in hedges, and even in turnip-fields,

and enjoyed excellent sport for the day; but on seeking, on the following morning, for a renewal of similar success, I have not found a single bird, the whole flight having proceeded on their course during the intervening night." We can hardly think these birds to be those alluded to by Mr. Julian, for the few hours' flight which would take them from the east coast to Devonshire could not reduce them from plump and well-conditioned birds to such as he describes.

In the spring emigration they are usually found congregating near the shore, preparatory to taking leave of us for a season. Many leave in February, and few remain after March, excepting those that remain to breed with us. These last would seem, nevertheless, to migrate as soon as the young ones have arrived at sufficient maturity, and again return with the regular flights in the autumn. Much yet remains to be elucidated in the history of this as well as many others of our migratory birds.

Like the Snipe, the Woodcock is very generally distributed in situations suited to its habits; but some districts are more favoured than others in the numbers that frequent them. So generally, indeed, are they distributed from the north of Scotland to the south of England, and from the east to the west, that any particular record of the various localities is quite unnecessary; but we will merely observe that in Ireland they are much more numerous than in either England or Scotland.

Out of this country, the Woodcock is found in Norway, Sweden, Lapland, Finland, Russia, Siberia, and Silesia. In France and Germany it is not common. It also occurs in Greece and Italy. In Northern Africa, they are found in Egypt and Barbary. In Madeira, they are said to be resident the whole year. In Asia, it occurs in India and Japan.

The habits of the Woodcock lead it to remain during the day in some secluded copse or wood, where it lies concealed, reposing under some holly or laurel bush, if such be attainable; or else under some spruce fir or brushwood, where the bottom is moist and clear. Unless disturbed, it remains in this concealment the whole day; but as twilight advances towards night, it leaves its day retreat on steady and silent wing for its feeding-ground, which is usually some marshy locality, often at a considerable distance. Night after night it follows the same well-known though unmarked track through some glade of the wood, returning with the first blush of day by the same road, which, from the circumstance of its being regularly frequented by these birds, obtains the name of 'cock-road,' or 'cock-shoot.' The period of twilight, when the Woodcock flies to and from its feeding-ground, is called by the Devonshire countrymen 'cock-light.'

During the day these birds may very frequently be found in hedgerows, particularly those which are wide, and open at the bottom; such situations should always be carefully examined and well beaten, for Woodcocks will often lie very close. Occasionally they will be found in very different situations; we remember once seeing one flushed in the middle of an elevated, open, stony, very dry grass-field, in the afternoon of a late October day; we should have rather looked for a Plover in such a locality. In districts where heathy mountains prevail, with woody glens interspersed here and there, they may often in open weather, particularly early in the season, be found taking shelter during the daytime among the heath; but woods are their favourite day retreat.

Singular as it may seem, there can now be no doubt of the fact, that Woodcocks carry their young, which are very helpless, from the nest to their night feeding-grounds; this was formerly thought to be effected by means of the feet. Mr. C. St. John, in elucidation of this point, writes: "Many people doubt the fact of the Woodcock carrying her young, from the wood to the swamp, in her feet; and certainly the claws of the Woodcock appear to be little adapted to grasping and carrying a heavy substance; yet such is most undoubtedly the case. Regularly, as the evening comes on, many Woodcocks carry their young ones down to the soft feeding-grounds, and bring them back again to the shelter of the woods before daylight, where they remain during the whole day. I myself have never happened to see the Woodcocks in the act of returning, but I have often seen them going down to the swamps in the evening, carrying their young with them. Indeed it is quite evident that they must in most instances transport the newly-hatched birds in this manner, as their nests are generally placed in dry heathery woods, where the young would inevitably perish unless the old ones managed to carry them to some more favourable feeding-ground.

"Snipes, Redshanks, and several other birds of this genus, are hatched and brought up on the same kind of ground on which they feed; but Woodcocks, in this country at least, are generally hatched far from the marshes, and therefore the old birds must of necessity carry their helpless young to these places, or leave them to starve in the dry heather; nor is the food of the Woodcock of such a nature that it could be taken to the young from the swamps in any sufficient quantity. Neither could the old birds bring with it the moisture necessary for the subsistence of all birds of this kind. In fact they have no means of feeding their young, except by carrying them to their food, for they cannot carry their food to them." The same fact has also been affirmed by several other observers, and Mr. St. John's personal testimony we conceive to be conclusive evidence of their doing so, though Gilbert White considered the feat improbable; yet it is surely less so than that asserted by Buffon, who says that they "take a weak one under their throat, and carry it more than a thousand paces." Bewick quotes this, and as he gives no other explanation or conjecture, it is to be supposed that he looked upon it as possible. "This curious habit," writes Sir R. Payne-Gallwey, "extraordinary as it may appear, has been observed by many sportsmen and naturalists, and is well vouched for. The precise mode in which the young are transported seems to vary. They are sometimes clutched up and carried in the feet, sometimes pressed between the thighs of the parent bird, or supported partly by the feet and partly by the bill."

Its method of feeding is by probing the soft, muddy ground with its long bill, the extremity of which is covered, as is also the case with all the birds of this genus, with an extremely sensitive membrane. Any worm which happens to be within reach of its bill becomes a sure victim; and the operation of probing is said by Daniels, who had the opportunity of seeing these birds in confinement, to be "performed in an instant, and the action of the Woodcock was so equal and imperceptible that it seemed doing nothing: it never missed its aim." The feeding-places of these birds may be detected by the small holes left by their borings, and the same ground is frequented night after night.

The flight of the Woodcock is, during the day, generally steady; and as it rises without much noise, it does not paralyse the young sportsman's nerves, as some of our other Game Birds do; and he consequently finds it not a very difficult shot, particularly where its flight is not impeded by trees or other obstacles. At night, when going to or returning from its feeding-grounds, its flight is very rapid, and its speed when endeavouring to escape imminent danger is extraordinarily quick.

The following account from a sporting publication is so interesting, that we quote it at length:—"It was growing towards evening, and I was about to return to the village of Golgate, when my attention was attracted by the rapid flight of two birds, one evidently pursuing the other. They had come from the higher and more hilly grounds, and when I first observed them, they were at a considerable distance. They approached and crossed in such a manner as to enable me to distinguish that the first was the small dark-coloured Woodcock, the second a very swift-winged bird, which appeared to be the Sparrow-Hawk; at all events it was a bird of prey, and I feel very little doubt that I am correct in its designation. The distance between the pursued and the pursuer might be about thirty yards; they crossed me at about three times that distance, which afforded a good view of this interesting struggle; the former was flying for life, the latter for a supper. The flight was direct; there was none of that turning and twisting which may be frequently observed when a small bird, in the presence of its merciless enemy, the Sparrow-Hawk, the Hobby, or the Merlin, endeavours to avoid or procrastinate its fate by twisting and dodging; on the contrary, the Woodcock continued his course, took the sea, followed by his fierce pursuer; and they both flew completely out of my sight. I kept my eyes in the same direction for some minutes, but I could observe the return of neither the Hawk nor the Woodcock; whether they were lost in the Channel, or reached the Sister Island, I cannot pretend to decide; but, as long as I could descry them, the bird of prey did not gain upon his intended victim."

I observed a Woodcock pursued by a Hawk on another occasion (in Delamere Forest, Cheshire), when, after a short space, the latter gave up the chase, and the Woodcock flew away. These are incontestible proofs of the extraordinary power and speed of this bird on the wing.

The Woodcock is monogamous.

Woodcocks are sometimes taken by horse-hair snares, which are set in intervals purposely left here and there in a little hedge, or wall of a few inches high, placed in its feeding-grounds; the bird, coming to this hedge, does not attempt to jump over it, but runs along till it comes to one of the openings, and in attempting to avail itself of this it is taken in the snare. Nets were also formerly used for the capture of these birds; an engraving of a springe for Woodcock and Snipe will be found in Sir R. Payne-Gallwey's "Fowler in Ireland."

The chief food of these birds is undoubtedly worms, and these are obtained, as we have before remarked, by probing the ground in soft, wet places. The old notion that the Woodcocks, as well as the Snipes, lived on 'suction,' is now quite exploded; though what was intended to be conveyed by the expression, we confess we never quite understood; but we suppose it must have referred to some very subtile and immaterial articles of diet. So far, however, from the Woodcock subsisting on such light and airy nothings, it consumes an incredible quantity of substantial, though easily assimilated food, of which small earth-worms form the staple. It also feeds on insects of various kinds; and one method in which it procures these is thus mentioned by the Rev. R. A. Julian, in *The Naturalist* (vol. iv. p. 78):—"I frequently noticed last season the fallen oak leaves disturbed in patches for some yards where I found these birds, and was at length highly gratified, whilst peeping over a bank, in seeing one taking up the leaves separately, and passing them, quick as thought, through its beak; thus clearing off the small insects that adhered to both sides." Add to these water beetles, and other aquatic insects, and a moderate quantity of vegetable matter, mostly *Confervæ*, which usually abound in the water in the feeding-places of these birds. Small pebbles are also generally found in the stomach.

The terms applied by sportsmen to these birds are as follow:—A couple, or a couple and a half, of Woodcocks; a greater number is called a fall or flight. In putting it up you are said to flush it; and it is then on the wing. When at rest they are fallen.

The dogs best calculated for beating for Woodcocks are small stout spaniels; for the fatigue of pushing through bushes and brambles for the whole of a sporting day is considerable, and very small slight dogs, though highly bred, are unequal to the work. In suitable localities, such as wooded glens, we have seen excellent sport secured by sending men with sticks, literally to "beat about the bushes." Should there be a road or pathway tolerably open, down the centre of the glen, you may be sure of pleasant shooting, if the woods contain any Cocks.

Messrs. D'Urban and Mathew, in "The Birds of Devon," remark that, "Most sportsmen who have shot Woodcocks must have had instances in their experiences of birds dropping as if dead to the shot, and then rising again and going off as if completely uninjured when an attempt was made to pick them up. In the game-larder at Lundy we had many couple of Cock deposited on the shelves, which had been shot on Christmas Eve, and none being wanted for the next day, the door was not opened until the morning of the 26th, when we heard screams proceeding from its neighbourhood, and found they came from the cook, who, on entering the larder, had discovered four or five of the Woodcocks 'come to life again,' and running about on the floor."

The sight of the Woodcock would seem to be not very acute in the daytime, at least when directed to any object immediately in front of it; this arises, probably, from the lateral position of the eyes. We quote the following anecdote, bearing on this point, from the paper by the Rev. R. A. Julian, already referred to :—" This season one flew against my breast; and last year another was observed by a friend of mine to knock itself down against a house, and when he came to the spot it was perfectly dead. I have heard my father relate an incident of one flying against a marker whom he had stationed in a tree, and striking him so severely on the cheek as to draw blood."

The following account of the shooting of a white Woodcock in Ireland, we take from *The Sportsman* magazine of July 1836, in which it appeared under the signature of "Cycyl" :—" My friend Captain St. Q——, well known in the Irish sporting circles, while quartered last year in Galway, in Ireland, was asked by Colonel Persse to join a party to shoot Woodcocks in the covers adjoining Clarum Bridge, saying at the same time that a white Woodcock had been seen occasionally; according to the report the country people made, it had visited these woods regularly every year for the four years past. I made inquiries to ascertain the fact of so singular a circumstance, and from every information I could collect, the fact was proved beyond a doubt.

"Taking advantage of a fall of snow—a time, it is well known to all sportsmen, all outlying Woodcocks are driven into the woods for shelter—a large party were asked, and assembled with alacrity, from the well-known excellence of the covers, abounding, as they do, with holly and arbutus. Each of the party had fully made up his mind that at least no exertions on his part should be wanting to bag the white Woodcock; and even if it should not be found, the day's sport would certainly be superb.

"On arriving at the ground, the snow still continued to fall, although not heavy, which, freezing as it fell, was of but little inconvenience to the party. The guns were stationed so as to give as small a chance of escape as possible to this 'rara avis,' if found. The first cover was closely beat, and although affording first-rate sport, still the object of every one's hopes and expectations had not appeared. While walking to the next cover, a passenger, judging solely from their long faces, would have laughed in his sleeve at the effect which the want of sport had upon the sportsmen's spirits.

"A few minutes' walk brought us to the next cover, abounding with that attractive canopy to Woodcock, the holly tree and the arbutus, which abundantly clothed both sides of an abrupt though short glen, giving an outlet for a spring which rises in the centre of the wood, surrounded by rocky elevations; on these the shooters chiefly took their stations. Captain St. Q—— had placed himself on the outside. Some of the beaters, having beat through to the end, were standing or lying about. No white Woodcock had appeared. The Captain with another of the party were moving off to the next cover, when one of the beaters, Cornelius O'Brien, all through the most sanguine about finding it, just peeped out of the cover, to see if, in his opinion, the guns were keeping a good look-out. To his dismay he saw Captain St. Q—— walking off, thinking the cover beat. Corny rushed at him, hallooing out, 'Oh! Captain, jewel! Oh, your honour, may the saints protecht ye; but ye have laved her behand ye. Oh! glory to your soul, come back and finish her. Och, is it to be laving her you are, after his honour's raising all the gintlemen in the country to kill her, and may be the crature dancing in her delight at desaving so many English gintlemen, for she's a 'cute little darling? I tell your honour the very best spot is laved, and it is I who ought to know it too. Oh! your honour will come back?'

"Who could have withstood this appeal? Captain St. Q—— returned, certainly not expecting to see the bird, notwithstanding all Corny had been saying.

"Corny went to the spot alluded to, hallooed out a few times, cock, cock, cock, hey cock, followed by a loud, deep —mark! mark! and an Irish screech that I cannot describe. Past went a bird like a white Pigeon—off went the gun— bang—bang—to make sure—whizz—and down it came, with a cheer from the beaters echoing through and through the wood, almost exceeding the exhilarating cheer when, after a long unsuccessful draw, a fox slips away over a fine country in full view of an almost hopeless field. Up Corny runs, stumbling over every impediment in his hurry, until he catches it; then, as proud as a duke, he walks with the bird in his hand up to the party, saying, 'Oh! your honour is the best shot in' the county of Galway, out and out; sure, your honour, that was an alegant shot! oh, it was indeed a fine shot; I would walk the world over, after your honour, shooting!' After the examination, Captain St. Q—— became the lion; a thousand questions were asked as to the exact position it was in when struck, such as a little up or down, flying to the right or left, &c., &c. In a short time each man had a different version of the fact; some hinted it was no remark-able shot; if they had been there, they could have killed it too; and certainly never could have mistaken it for a white Pigeon, for really that was too ridiculous.

"But the death of the white Woodcock does not, as you may suppose, rest here. All the old men and women attribute their ill luck this season to the death of the 'good bird' (fairy). Cornelius, too, has been but badly off since; his crop of potatoes, on which he had placed so much consequence, from the appearance of the stalk, on getting up, proved to be a complete failure; and, to sum up all, his wife, a sweet, pretty creature, the beauty of the barony and the adjoining ones, with eyes like sloes, snow-white teeth, and a beautiful figure, has been brought to bed of an idiot — all through Corny having been one of the murderers of the 'good bird' who had protected the barony from all harm these four years back.

"Ould Widdie O'Reilly has said, 'In one more season Corny will want for a pratie,' and 'the ould divil is too demented to say what is not true,' at least so Father O'Toole says.

"To those who know Ireland, this will not appear extraordinary; to others I must beg to assure them this is quite the feeling of the Irish. That Corny will want is beyond a doubt; for there exists, although quite unintentionally, a sort of superstitious combination against him. But having no faith in these things myself, I have now only to say that the bird was rather large, milk white, with the exception of two brown feathers in the right wing, and one in the left; the beak brown, and the legs grey. The eyes were what is termed 'wall-eyed' in horses; the condition was excellent.

"The bird is stuffed in the best style, and in the possession of Colonel Persse, of Galway, and any person, by making a proper application, I dare say, will be allowed to see it."

The time of pairing is somewhat uncertain, but it is probably very early in the spring; some think that pairing takes place before they leave our shores, but this seems to be doubtful, unless among those that are late in migrating. A considerable number of these birds annually remain to breed with us; and from the infrequency of such records formerly, we are obliged to conclude that some unknown general cause has of late years been in operation which has led them to remain here to breed. What this cause may be, no one seems to know; it possibly may be that the extensive forests in the north of Europe may not now offer as secure and quiet a retreat as formerly; indeed we have heard that for some years past their eggs have been eagerly sought after and exposed in the markets in Sweden for sale. Whether this has been carried on to a sufficient extent to induce the birds to seek other nesting-places, we are not able to state; we merely mention the fact.

The nest of the Woodcock is placed on the ground, and is composed wholly of dead leaves, such as those of the ferns. It is built in some dry situation in a wood, often among long grass, but where there is little underwood; or among heath, which is sometimes found in open, elevated woods. Mr. C. St. John states that the nests are found in Sutherlandshire, "not only in the large fir plantations, but also in the smaller patches of birch, &c., which fringe the shores of many of the most northern lakes." "As I have seen their nests at all times from March to August, it is natural to suppose that the Woodcock breeds more than once in the season."

During the pairing time the Woodcock has a peculiar call-note, which Mr. Lloyd, in his work on the Game Birds of Scandinavia, describes as follows:—"During its morning and evening flights, at this time the Woodcock gives utterance to a peculiar call-note which sportsmen express by *knort, knort, knisp*, or more properly, perhaps, *orrt, orrt, pisp*. The first *knort* or *orrt* is a hollow coarse and somewhat lengthened nasal sound; the second *knisp* or *pisp*, a short fine and sharp sort of whistle which, when one is accustomed to it, may be heard at a considerable distance. This note clearly appears to be one by which the betrothed invite each other to pairing; for the bird seems to pay very little attention to the *orrt*, but always listens and looks about it as soon as it hears the *pisp*."

The eggs, which are four in number, vary in the ground colour from creamy buff to dark stone buff, with spots and blotches of dull purplish brown or dark brown, and two shades of reddish yellow brown at the broader end. They measure in length one inch and three-quarters, by one inch and a third in breadth. The time occupied in incubation is believed by Mr. Creighton to be twenty-one days; and he states that the young leave the nest immediately after birth, and that

the male bird remains in the neighbourhood of the nest
during the time of incubation.

When the following accounts were written, the nesting
of the Woodcock in this country was regarded as a very rare
occurrence, though becoming more frequent than formerly :—
Mr. W. C. Williamson has recorded, in Loudon's *Magazine
of Natural History*, the occurrence of three pairs breeding
"in one wood belonging to Mr. Francis Hurt, Alderwasley,
near Derby. The nests, when discovered, all contained eggs,
the old birds being then sitting. I wrote to Mr. Hurt on
April 29th (1836), requesting him to procure for our society
a nest with eggs ; and two or three days after, he kindly sent
me the nest, with the broken shells of four eggs, which, as
well as those of the other nests, had been hatched even at
that early period of the year. Two of the young broods,
with the old birds leading them about, have been seen by
the gamekeeper of that gentleman, who remarks in his letter,
that on going to the nest, the old bird did not rise until he
had approached within the distance of a yard. They were
all in dry, warm situations, amongst dead grass and leaves,
without any attempt at concealment. The nest sent was
wholly composed of dead leaves, chiefly of the common fern,
loosely laid together, and without any lining. The underwood was thin, and of not more than from seven to ten years'
growth."

The Rev. W. T. Bree, in 1828, collected a number of
instances of the Woodcock breeding in this country. Two
young ones were shot on May 19th, 1828, near Nuneaton.
A nest and four eggs were found in Ryton Wood, near
Coventry, early in May 1827, but were deserted. Woodcocks were shot on April 9th, 1828, in some woods near
Nuneaton. Three other instances are also mentioned, as
quoted from the local papers.

We give the above as being some of the earliest records
on this subject ; the list might now very readily be greatly
extended, but we shall merely observe that Woodcocks' nests
are by no means very rare in many districts in the north,

and that they have occurred repeatedly even in the extreme south in Dorset and Devon, and more or less frequently in nearly all the intervening counties.

The Woodcock readily submits to confinement; in *The Naturalist*, the Rev. R. A. Julian says: "My father informs me, a bird of this species, which had been pinioned, was kept alive for several years at Widey Court, about three miles from this town (Plymouth); it suffered, however, severely in dry summers, and was only sustained by strips of raw meat, placed in a pan with mud. At other times it managed to shift for itself pretty well."

Woodcocks vary much both in size and colour, depending probably on the effects of age or sex, or both; some sportsmen contend that there are three species, or at least varieties, and specify the common ash-coloured one, the small red bird, and the large black or dark one: these, however, are all referable to the one species varied by age or sex. The Rev. G. F. Dawson, in the *Zoologist*, has thus alluded to one of the varieties, and as the subject is one of some interest, we extract it, leaving it to future observers to decide the point :—

"That there is a small variety of this bird (which may eventually prove a distinct species), I have long been aware, as many sportsmen must be also; but it has never, I believe, been generally noticed. Latham, indeed, speaks of two varieties of the common bird, and even describes three, but mentions them more as occasional deviations, than as possessing any permanent points of difference; yet the distinctive characters of the smaller bird in question are beyond what we should ordinarily assign to an accidental variety. It is more local, it is true, in its distribution; but independently of its smaller size, which alone would form no criterion whereby to judge of its distinctness from the Common Woodcock, which is well known to vary in size and weight most astonishingly; it possesses several other characteristics, which at once clearly distinguish it. In the family of *Scolopacidæ* generally, the females are not only larger than the males, but also of a darker plumage; the dark shades on the upper part of the back of the Common Woodcock, for instance, being blacker, and the red of the lower portion of a deeper red in the females than in the males; but in this small variety the colour of the males is much darker than that of any females of the common sort; in fact, it is known in some parts of the country by the name of the Little Black Cock. It differs also in its flight, by which it may be distinguished before it is brought to the ground by the fowling-piece of the sportsman; whereas the common bird generally springs with a noise which sometimes almost rivals that of the hen Pheasant. This bird, on the contrary, rises silently, and flies off in a sort of wavy or zigzag direction, a good deal like a Snipe, and with a flap of the wing as noiseless as that of an Owl; and indeed, I recollect, on one occasion, several years ago, when having killed one, I believed so confidently that I had been shooting at an Owl of some rare species, that was to prove to me a prize, that when I picked up my bird I was surprised to find it a Woodcock, forgetting, at the moment, the usual peculiar flight of this Little Black Cock."

Other varieties, which may be considered accidental, are not very uncommon; thus we find in addition to the pure white variety, which we have already noticed, others on record in which the general colour is much lighter, more approaching to a cream-colour, or pale ash. These do not, however, require special notice, and several are mentioned by Bewick in his " British Birds."

The bill, which is dark brown at the tip, shading towards the base into pale brownish pink, is about three inches in length; eyes, large and prominent; irides, dark brown; orbits, pale buff. The forehead, and as far as the centre of the head, grey; from thence to the nape are four blackish brown transverse bands, separated by narrow bars of light yellowish brown; from the gape to the eye is a stripe of rich brown; cheeks, pale yellowish brown, with dark brown spots. Under the ear coverts is a band of dark brown;

chin, pale yellowish brown ; front of neck, breast, and belly, yellow brown, barred transversely with darker brown. The upper parts are prettily variegated with grey brown, pale ochre, and red brown with some dark brown markings. These colours are disposed in a variety of ways, in spots, bars, and streaks, and otherwise mottled ; but as a very lengthy description would be requisite in order to give these with accuracy, we shall content ourselves with this general description, and refer to our plate, which will give all requisite information. Primaries, black brown, the outer webs marked with triangular spots of reddish brown ; the outer web of the first primary is usually of a lighter colour than that of the other quills, and often it will be entirely destitute of dark markings ; some sportsmen consider this to indicate a female ; others, a male ; it, however, appears to be a very uncertain guide, occurring as often in one sex as in the other, being simply a characteristic of age ; the dark markings gradually disappearing from the base to the tip as the bird becomes older. The tail consists of twelve feathers, which are black, but tipped with grey ; underneath the tips are pure white ; the upper tail coverts only allow about three-quarters of an inch of the tail to be seen. The legs are short, feathered to the knees, of a brownish flesh-colour ; claws, black.

The female has the feathers on the upper part of the back blacker, and those on the lower part redder, than the male Woodcock. She is also always larger.

The young birds have the bill shorter than the adult.

Few birds vary more in weight than Woodcocks. The ordinary weight of the adult male is from eleven to twelve ounces ; the females will often weigh from fourteen to sixteen ounces ; the latter weight is, however, by no means usual. Mr. Yarrell, on the authority of Lady Peyton, records one shot in 1775 or 1776 which was of the extraordinary weight of twenty-seven ounces ; and another, obtained some years previously, which weighed twenty-four ounces.

As a bird for the table, the Woodcock is greatly and

almost universally esteemed; the ordinary selling price is high for so small a bird—a sufficient proof of the estimation in which they are held by gourmets. They are frequently dressed with the trail or intestines in, an unpleasant idea to those who object to eat the semi - digested earth-worms, which constitute their chief good.

BIBLIOGRAPHY.

Messrs. D'URBAN and MATHEW, in "The Birds of Devon," give a very interesting account of the Woodcock in Devon, which county is one of their favourite resorts in winter.

Mr. HARTING, in the *Zoologist* for Nov. 1879, gives an interesting account of the transport of the young, with a sketch by Wolf.

Sir RALPH PAYNE-GALLWEY, in "The Fowler in Ireland," gives a full account of the pursuit of the Woodcock in that country.

THE GREAT SNIPE

SOLITARY SNIPE—DOUBLE SNIPE.

Gallinago major, ... GMELIN.

Gallinago—From *Gallina*—A hen. *Major*—Greater.

Grande Bécassine, French; *Narseja grande*, Portuguese; *Agachadixa real*, Spanish; *Croccolone*, Italian; *Bekkach-ta-meja*, Maltese; *Doppelschneppe, grosser Sumpfschneppe*, German; *Poelsnip*, Dutch; *Tredækkare*, Danish; *Dobbelt-bekkasin*, Norwegian; *Dubbel Beccasin*, Swedish; *Heinäkurppa*, Finnish; *Leshnenok*, Russian.

THE Great or Solitary Snipe is only a straggling visitor to these islands from the high northern latitudes in which it breeds. By far the greater number of specimens have been obtained in the autumn and early winter months, and these would seem to be merely stragglers from the great body which migrate to winter in Africa, in which continent it occurs as far south as Natal.

In England they occur not uncommonly in Norfolk, as stated by Mr. Yarrell, on the authority of the Rev. R. Lubbock, who says, "I have known more than twenty specimens come under my own observation in the same season; but I cannot remember a single instance where this Snipe has occurred in spring: I have made many inquiries, and have invariably found them occurring in autumn, generally early in the season, often in September." The Reverends A. and H. Matthews have recorded that "a few specimens of the Great Snipe have at different times been killed in this part of the country (Oxfordshire). The last of these

was shot on the banks of the Isis, close to the city of
Oxford, in 1839, by a servant of Worcester College." The
time of the year is not mentioned. They have also been
shot in Wales, Cornwall, Devonshire, Oxfordshire, Kent,
Lincolnshire, and Lancashire, and probably in many other
counties; but in Scotland it is very rare.

In Ireland they have been frequently procured, and a
number of instances are recorded by Mr. Thompson; who,
however, considers it a rare visitor. We make the following
extract from his valuable work, relating to the occurrence of
this bird in the county of Wexford :—" In November 1836,
Captain (now Major) T. Walker, of Belmont, Wexford, wrote
to me respecting the occasional occurrence of the Solitary
Snipe in that county, where he had not, however, met with
it since 1830 or 1831. Being farther questioned, that gentleman replied in July 1846 :—' The Solitary Snipe I have at
different times shot here, is much larger than the Common
Snipe; bill, shorter; plumage, nearly alike, with the exception
of the belly, which in the Common is white, but in the Solitary
is speckled with grey and brown. It lies close, and when
flushed, makes no cry, flies steadily without twisting, and
slower than the Common (probably from its fatness, and not
being a shy bird), and pitches again, like the Jack Snipe,
after a short flight of thirty or forty yards. I never heard a
cry from it; but sportsmen abroad have told me it has one,
not, however, resembling that of the Common Snipe. I
believe that every year several come over, though not found
by sportsmen, who do not know where to look for them ;—
not in bogs, but in *long-grass* fields, in marshy neighbourhoods.
They frequent these abroad, and are called *Meadow* Snipe
(*Wiesen-schnepfe*). They breed in the marshes of Hungary,
and, being migratory, come to the marshy district between
Laibach and Upper Laibach, long before any frost could
influence their flight. They remain there not more than a
fortnight, and I know from sportsmen, are soon afterwards
found in quantities in the Pontine marshes. The Double
Snipe of the Continent is the same as the bird I have killed

in Ireland. In one winter, about fifteen years ago, Solitary Snipes were plentiful in the grassy lands of Hayestown, at the foot of the mountain of Forth, about four miles from Wexford. Every day I shot there, I got three or four birds; since that time the ground has been drained, and all kinds of Snipe have quitted it; but I generally get a few elsewhere in the course of the winter's shooting in the county of Wexford.'"

It breeds in the extreme north of Europe, and extends from Scandinavia to the valley of the Yenesay. It has been obtained at Trebizond, and in the Caucasus on its migration.

The Great Snipe approaches in some of its habits and manners to the Jack Snipe, rather than to the Common Snipe. When flushed, it flies but a short distance, and then settles again; it rises without any cry, and flies much more heavily and steadily than the Common Snipe, and is consequently an easy mark for the sportsman. Should he, however, wish to follow out and enjoy the shooting and eating these birds, he must proceed to Sweden, where, Mr. Greiff states, that fifty or sixty may be killed in one day, particularly in autumn, when they are extremely fat. This fatness has been remarked upon by nearly all those who have been fortunate in meeting them in any numbers, and their heavy flight has been attributed to this cause. Their haunts are said to be somewhat different to those of the Common Snipe, being long-grass, marshy fields, and not bogs. By far the greatest number of birds shot in this country are young birds of the year; but we have seen a fine old specimen, which had been procured in Ireland; the locality we could not ascertain. The breast and abdomen of this specimen were more white, and had fewer of the dark markings than in any other Great Snipe we have ever met with. Though called solitary, it seems in countries frequented by it in any numbers, to be generally found in pairs. When flying it is said to spread the tail like a fan.

It is monogamous.

Mr. Greiff states that it has a peculiar note at the breeding-season, and "commences with a sound resembling the smack of the tongue, and thereupon four or five louder follow."

The food of the Great Snipe is said by Sir Humphry Davy to be the larvæ of the Daddy Long Legs; in scientific language, *Tipulæ*. These are very abundant in meadows, and are exceedingly injurious to the roots of the grass on which they subsist: this may in some measure account for these birds frequenting meadows, where their favourite food is so plentiful.

In Sweden the shooting of the Great Snipe commences in July, and may be pursued till the end of September.

The nest is very simple, consisting of a little dry grass, or other marshy plants; it is placed in some slight depression in the ground by the side of a tuft of coarse grass or rushes. The eggs are four in number, and are spotted with two shades of red brown upon a yellow olive brown ground. They measure one inch and three-quarters in length, by one inch and a sixth in breadth. Incubation is usually completed by the end of May, or early in June.

In the adult the bill is of a pale yellowish brown, with dark brown tip, and is about two inches and a half long; irides, dark brown; forehead and crown, dark brown, divided in the centre from before backwards by a streak of pale brown, and bounded on each side over the eye and ear coverts by a similar pale streak. From the beak to the eye is a streak of dark brown. Chin, pale yellowish brown; neck, pale brown, each feather with a darker centre. The upper parts are varied, as in the other Snipes, with black and blackish brown, streaked, margined, and tipped with buff and white, but which it is not easy to convey a correct impression of by words. Quills, grey black, with the shafts white; secondaries, black, tipped with white; tertials, black, barred and streaked with pale brown; rump feathers, dark brown, with pale edgings; upper tail coverts, pale wood brown, with darker markings. The tail consists of sixteen feathers; the centre eight black, with a chestnut tip, terminated with a narrow bar of black and white; the four outer feathers on each side are white, with some black bars on the outer webs; the whole much concealed by the coverts.   Breast and sides, pale ochreous, marked with crescentic bands of black; belly and vent, yellowish white.   The legs and toes would seem to vary considerably; Mr. Yarrell having seen them of a livid green and light drab in fresh specimens.

The female is larger, and darker in her markings, than the male.

The young birds may be known by the tail having the four white outside feathers barred as in the Common Snipe, and in having the bill short.   The under part of the plumage is darker than in the adult bird.

In weight the male reaches to seven or eight ounces; the female, to nine.

The length from the tip of the bill to the end of the tail is about twelve inches.   The expanse of the wings is about eighteen inches.

The plate is taken from a drawing by Mr. John Gatcombe, of Plymouth.   The specimen from which it was drawn was procured in the neighbourhood of Plymouth.

They are said to be "most delicious eating," and are dressed in the same way as Woodcock and the other Snipes, with the trail in.

BIBLIOGRAPHY.

Mr. SEEBOHM, in his " British Birds," gives an interesting account of the habits of this species as observed by him on the banks of the Petchora.

THE SNIPE

WHOLE SNIPE—FULL SNIPE—HEATHER-BLEATER.

Gallinago cælestis .   .   .   .   .   LINNÆUS.

Gallinago—From *Gallina*—A hen.
Cælestis—Coming from heaven.

Bécassine, French ; *Narseja,* Portuguese ; *Agachadisa, Agachona,*
Spanish ; *Beccaccino reale,* Italian ; *Choseh,* Arabic ; *Bou-monkar,*
Moorish ; *gemeine Schnepfe, Moorschnepfe,* German ; *Watersnip,*
Dutch ; *Dobbelt Bekkasin,* Danish ; *Mujresnujpa,* Færoese ; *Hros-
sagaukur, Myrisnipa,* Icelandic ; *Enkelt-Bekkasin, Raagjeit,* Nor-
wegian ; *Enkel - Beckasin, Horsgök,* Swedish ; *Taivaan - vuohi,*
Finnish ; *Bekass, Barachék,* Russian.

THE Common Snipe is well known to every sportsman,
being very generally distributed over the whole country;
and in some districts, where haunts suited to its wants and
habits are found, it exists in great numbers. Although a
very considerable body, greater perhaps than is generally
supposed, remains with us throughout the year, breeding in
our marshy heaths in the spring, yet there is no doubt that
a very large accession to their numbers is received during
the autumn months; and again in the spring the great body
disappears for more suitable localities for incubation than this
country commonly affords.

Out of this country its geographical range is very great.
It frequents the whole of the north of Europe and Asia.
Seebohm, in a note to his most interesting work, "Siberia in
Europe," says : "The Common Snipe breeds throughout the

Arctic and sub-Arctic regions of Europe and Asia, from the British Islands eastwards to the Pacific. It winters in various parts of Southern Europe, Persia, India, and China."

The haunts chiefly selected by the Common Snipe are the margins of marshy places, moist meadows, peaty bogs, and commons; the edges of small, tiny rivulets; little open ditches in fields; and very often ploughed lands. Severe frost will, however, frequently drive it to places where we should hardly expect to find it; thus we remember on one occasion springing a Snipe on the sea-shore, not in a muddy, soft place, but on the small shingle, at the edge of the water; apparently seeking its food as the Dunlin and Ring Dotterel do. When you spring a Snipe, it manifests the greatest reluctance to fly with the wind, and in fact never does so more than a few yards, when it turns, and after several 'tacks,' or zigzag movements of great rapidity, it goes off in the teeth of the wind. The Snipe is generally considered a difficult shot, but this arises, in a great measure, from the sportsman firing at it during its zigzag flight, when the chances of hitting it are extremely small. The proper time to fire is either immediately the bird is off the ground, and before it has commenced its eccentric movements, or else just after it has concluded, and is commencing its proper and steady flight.

In beating for Snipe, the sportsman should always endeavour to spring them down wind, for the bird, of course, flies off at first down the wind, but immediately commences flying against it, which it accomplishes, as before stated, by a series of 'tacks;' and by the time these are over, and its flight is steady, it will seldom be out of your reach, but will generally present a fair side-shot for your gun. During wet or windy weather the Snipe will not lie well, but is usually very wild. To enjoy Snipe-shooting to advantage, the weather must be still and calm; on such days the birds lie closely, and will rise well within shot. To aid in finding the Snipe, a good pointer or setter is desirable. When a Snipe is shot, it very frequently happens that, in walking up to the dead Snipe, another is put up, which, if the sportsman is unprepared, escapes.

The Snipe is generally considered a solitary bird in its habits, and it is urged in proof of this, that where they abound, and are put up in large flocks, they instantly scatter, and do not fly off in a body. This is true, as to the fact, as we have several times witnessed in Ireland; but we should be inclined to look upon their scattering, under such circumstances, as a preservative instinct, rather than as a proof that they are unsociable birds. We hazard this conjecture from having, on many occasions, in the south-west of Dorsetshire, seen small flocks of Snipe, numbering from twenty to thirty or forty birds in each, flying in a body when not frightened, and continuing together as long as they kept in view. This was generally late in autumn, or early in winter.

The following remarks on the habits of this bird, by the late Mr. Thompson, are so much to the purpose, that we venture to give them entire :—" I have myself had some experience in Snipe-shooting, and can truly say, that of all our birds, Snipes seem to be the most sensible to the skyey influences; or possibly what appears to us their sensibility, may be prompted by their instinctive knowledge of that of the minute creatures on which they prey;—the successful pursuit of these may require the frequent change of ground. Bogs, under similar circumstances of weather, at least to our senses, will exhibit their thirty or forty brace of Snipe one day, and not more than three or four brace the next. The birds would seem to be almost ever on the move from one locality to another. At the dusk of every evening, too, they leave their more retired daily haunts, chiefly to feed in localities where they would be disturbed during the day. At such times any little moist place invites them ;—two low, excavated portions within the grounds of the Royal Academical Institution, in the town of Belfast, were at one time (and may be still) nightly visited. We generally meet with them at the 'witching hour' on flight from the higher to the lower grounds; but when I have been walking on the mountains in the autumnal evenings, they have passed over my head on their way from the valley towards the mountain-top. We can hardly walk anywhere about the town just named (Belfast) in the autumnal or winter days, and sometimes even in those of summer, when becoming dusk, without hearing the call of the Snipe on the way to its nightly quarters.

" It is an extremely interesting sight to witness these birds coming in numbers to favourite night feeding-grounds, such as the 'bog meadows,' already mentioned; when stationed on the ditch banks intersecting them, awaiting 'the flying' of Wildfowl—Ducks, Wigeon, Teal, &c.—one hears a continual concert kept up by Snipes coming at the commencement of twilight from the higher grounds—their places of refuge for the day—and alighting all around, the call ceasing the moment they touch the earth. For an instant only in the twilight are they seen, and then with downward pointed bill, they have a most singular appearance as they sometimes come falling, apparently from the clouds, close around us. Notwithstanding their proximity, the flight being over, a perfect stillness reigns, until we fire a shot, which alarms them, and those very near us take wing. Should the moon 'show forth her silver lining to the night,' it is the signal for them to move about from one part of the meadows to another, calling all the while they are on flight. During moonlight, too, in particular, they feed much in some districts in stubble and other fields. When shore-shooting on moonlight nights, I have raised Snipes from the edge of the flowing tide in Belfast Bay. The Wildfowl-shooters state that during autumn and winter numbers of Snipes disperse themselves to feed every evening, but more especially by moonlight, over the extensive banks of *Zostera*, exposed by the retiring tide from either shore to the edge of the channel, along which also they may sometimes be observed feeding like ordinary shore-birds. One of my informants killed three at a shot on these banks by moonlight. They are not sought for here by shooters, but make known their presence by their peculiar cry when they rise on wing; very rarely a few remain during the day. About the little grassy pools on a low bank, over which the tide always flows at extreme high water, these birds have frequently been noticed. From all the low-lying night feeding-grounds visited in the manner described, they commonly take their leave very early in the morning; a few lazy ones, however, remaining until molested, when they fly direct to their upland or retired haunts."

A writer in Loudon's *Magazine of Natural History* for 1829, states that "in the latter end of October, and during the month of November, great numbers frequent the broads (or river-lakes) with which this county (Norfolk) abounds. They rest on beds of water-cresses, and the broken remains of the *Scirpus lacustris* (which had previously been cut by the marshmen, under the name of bolders, for chair-bottoms), and the *Typha latifolia* (*vulgo*, Gladdon), and *Sparganium ramosum* (*vulgo*, Black-weed), which are used by coopers to put between the staves of casks. On the floating remains of these and other aquatic plants, they lie in great numbers, and are to be approached only by the means of a boat. In the early part of a morning when the whiteness of a hoar-frost renders the Snipes visible, the marshmen secrete themselves in a small boat behind a neighbouring reed-bush, and shoot at them sitting upon these broken weeds, and have sometimes the good fortune to kill many at a shot. In the latter part of November they gradually take their departure, and, except a few stragglers, arc not to be met with before the months of February and March, in the following spring."

Snipes are monogamous, and pairing takes place very early, occasionally as soon as the end of February, or beginning of March, but usually not till the end of the latter month, or early in April; at which time the male Snipe serenades his mate with two distinct notes, differing as widely from each other as from the cry they utter at other times. The one note may be compared to the repetition of the word 'tinker, tinker,' uttered in a sharp, shrill tone, as the bird ascends in its flight; the other, uttered as he descends, is somewhat similar to the bleating of a lamb, only in a deeper tone, and accompanied with a violent vibration of the wings. It is from this latter note that the Snipe derives its name of Heather-bleater; and various conjectures have been made as to the way in which it is produced by the bird; some high authorities in matters ornithological—as Selby, Macgillivray, &c.—considering that it is produced by some peculiar vibration of the wings; others look upon it as effected by the vocal organs; but the former opinion is undoubtedly correct, as it may be produced by tying the expanded wings of the bird on to a stick and passing them rapidly through the air.

The more common note, and one which is heard whenever a Snipe is sprung, has been compared to the word 'chissick,' repeated with a lisp. On such occasions it is the note of alarm, but it is also used at other times when the bird is undisturbed.

The old notion that Snipes lived by suction is now quite exploded; something far more substantial than anything attainable by that process, falls to their lot. The bill of the Snipe is one of the most beautifully contrived structures that can well be imagined, and is most admirably adapted to its necessities and mode of procuring food. If the beak is soaked in water for a few days, the cuticle, or outside skin, will readily peel off, and the beak itself will be exhibited. The enlarged end of this will be found to be most beautifully reticulated; having numerous elevated lines enclosing six-sided cells. The object of this curious provision is, there can be no doubt, to afford a greater surface for the expansion of the nervous filaments which supply the beak with sensation; the beak, particularly at the extremity, being thus rendered extremely sensitive to the slightest external impression, is able to detect worms and other animals when below the surface of the ground, where a large portion of the Snipe's food is obtained, and which could never be procured were it dependent on its eyes only for finding the creatures on which it feeds.

In procuring its food, the Snipe forces its bill into the soft, muddy ground, to a greater or less depth; sometimes even the whole bill will be immersed, as is proved by seeing mud on the feathers of the forehead of dead birds; the delicately sensitive skin which covers the beak, and forms a nervous cushion at the end, instantly betrays any unfortunate worm or other creature that may come in contact with it,

and it is instantly seized and eaten. In this way it picks up
most of its food, and as Snipes are very generally in most
excellent condition, we may infer that it finds little difficulty
in procuring an ample supply of insect life. Digestion appears to be very rapidly accomplished, for frequently but little
is found in the stomach, if examined—the powerful gizzard
and gastric juice having ground up and dissolved the last-
taken food. At different times the following digestible items
have been found in their mouths or stomachs :—Worms of
all kinds and sizes; caterpillars of beetles and other insects;
small shell-snails; some vegetable substances; small seeds of
one of the sedges or reeds; other small seeds; and two
instances are mentioned by Mr. Thompson, in which a full-
grown horseleech was found in the stomach. Add to these
numerous small pieces of stone or gravel, and a good idea
of the substances picked up by the Snipes may be formed.

In sporting phraseology, we say of Snipes that we spring
them when we put them up; we talk of a couple, or a couple
and a half of Snipes; and when in small flocks we say a
wisp of Snipes.

It is a well-known fact that Snipes, and indeed, we believe,
all wild birds, are fatter and in better condition after a few
days' frost, than either before or after its lengthened continuance. Sir H. Davy's idea that this arose from their
haunting only warm springs at such times, where worms
are abundant, cannot be the case—at least we venture to
think so. We are inclined to look upon this fact, with
White, of Selbourne, as depending upon the slight check
which the insensible perspiration receives on such occasions,
and which, we believe, produces the effect named.

"When it is almost impossible to see a Snipe on the
ground by day, however close, how doubly hard it is, even
on a clear night, may easily be imagined. During severe
frost I have, through curiosity, crept up to springs on a
mountain side, where I knew many Snipe lay within a few
square yards, and, though gifted with excellent sight, could
rarely see one. A few steps nearer, and a 'wisp' of ten

or twelve would rise screaming. On one occasion I brought a powerful glass to bear on such a spot at a distance of some thirty paces. I could then count seven, some standing hunch-backed and motionless, others squatted on the dried grass, looking no bigger than mice or frogs. On flinging a stone at the spot, this time at least fifteen sprang. The next visit I paid was with a gun, when I fired on chance, guessing their position, and killed five, though I saw none. The peasantry and fowlers, by constant practice, bag many Snipe during frost by creeping up to the springs. They admit, however, that it is usual to kill more than they see when pulling the trigger. These men also wait in concealment near the wet places where Snipe feed, and shoot them singly as they come. On moonlight nights, their plan is to put a white feather into the ground, in a favourite spot the birds are known to frequent, and when Snipe alight they fire a dose of the smallest shot at the mark, now and then obtaining two or three of those feeding near. The movements of Snipe are more influenced by the moon than might be supposed. Though they will be found in plenty during the time of bright nights, as the moon wanes, their numbers diminish daily in their usual haunts. In many districts, when the nights are dark, the local shooters consider it a waste of time to seek them by day."

Incubation is completed at an early period; the gentleman from whom we have quoted above, states that he has shot "young Snipes, strong on the wing, as early as the last week in May." Mr. Thompson mentions young Snipes being sprung as early as the 18th of April, on the Belfast mountains, in 1832. These are certainly very early dates for young Snipes to be so far advanced as to be able to fly, and they will seldom be found in that condition much before the middle of June, except when the spring has been unusually early and mild. On such occasions it is probable there will be two broods reared the same year.

As soon as the young birds are excluded from the egg, they are able to run about, and follow the mother.

The nest of the Snipe is usually placed under some tuft of grass or sedge, upon some little piece of raised ground or hillock, where it will be free from moisture; it consists of a slight excavation, with a few dried blades of grass or heath as a lining. In this are deposited usually four eggs, but rarely five. These are in colour of pale greenish or yellowish white, mottled at the larger end with brown of two or three shades. They measure in length one inch and a half, by one inch and one line in breadth.

The Snipe may be readily tamed, and Dr. C. Cogswell, of Warrington, gives the following interesting account of one which he kept for some time in captivity:—"On Friday, the 30th of October 1847, while some men were out in the fields, in this neighbourhood, amusing themselves with catching small birds with a fly-net, they secured a full-grown Snipe, which came into my possession on the following day. The head was partially denuded of feathers, in consequence of the bird having struggled against the bars of a cage, through impatience at being confined. However, it made no effort to escape when held in the hand, and would even stand quietly on the knee, drink water out of a glass, and fish up worms from the bottom. I have now had this singular pet for more than two months, and, to all appearance, it is perfectly reconciled to its novel mode of life. During the late continuance of severe frost, there seemed every probability of its dying of hunger, as earth-worms were not to be procured; and, like the specimen noticed by Mr. Yarrell, it at first refused to take any other kind of nourishment; however, necessity soon prevailed, insomuch that the raw flesh of the hare and rabbit, together with tripe cut into narrow strips, have been taken into favour, but the ordinary kinds of butcher's meat are rejected. Earthworms remain decidedly the favourite article of diet, and of these it consumes a quart in three or four days. The habits of this creature are surprisingly familiar, considering its commonly-supposed irreclaimable nature. During the night it reposes quietly in a cage, standing on one leg, with the head under the wing. By day, however, a desire to be enlarged is signified by an incessant striking of the bill and head against its prison wires. When released, it flies about the rooms and passages, walks on the table, is pleased at being noticed by those about him, and is on terms of great intimacy with a little spaniel lap-dog. No situation seems to accord so well with the animal's ideas of comfort as a place on a stool before the fire. Thus accommodated to its liking, and especially if at the same time fondled with the voice and hand, or enjoying the close proximity of its canine associate, it emits a subdued whistling note, sometimes, but very rarely, varied with an approach to a twitter. The food is usually given to it in a glass of water. Wherever the vessel is placed, all that is requisite to secure prompt attendance is to scrape against the edge with a metallic substance. In feeding, it has great difficulty in seizing a worm, or any substance of similar form, that may happen to be lying on a flat surface. After repeated unsuccessful attempts, the morsel is at last got lengthwise between the mandibles, and disappears.

"Strangers are readily distinguished from the people of the house, as shown by an evident difference of manner, indicative of alarm, manifested in their presence. Should any one be too rude in his advances, the bird, in endeavouring to avoid him, has a peculiar way of erecting the tail feathers, and turning them all in the opposite direction. It likes to be kept clean, and devotes frequent attention to the smooth and orderly appearance of the plumage. Although, in the opinion, at least, of Milne Edwards, the visage of the birds of the genus bears the stamp of stupidity (*Leur aspect dénote la stupidité*), some of the foregoing circumstances indicate the possession of as large a share of intelligence on the part of the present convert to civilisation, as most of the feathered race are capable of testifying, by their actions, to our apprehension."

Varieties of the Snipe frequently occur; they are often of a white or cream colour, either plain, or mottled with light brown. Mr. Thompson records a curious variety, which had several times fallen under his notice :— " In the winter of 1831–32, several crested Snipes were shot in the bogs near the town just named (Belfast), by three of my sporting acquaintances, to the gun of one of whom two or three fell on the same day in the King's Moss. The crest of one which came under my inspection, extended for nine lines from the lower portion of the entire back of the head in a horizontal manner. Close to the head only, the feathers were brown and black, all the rest being white ; this crest arose from a warty protuberance. It is extraordinary that so many with crests should occur about the same time, as I had not before, nor have I since met with any but a single individual (in December 1841) having such an appendage. This specimen exhibited a row of feathers projecting in a drooping manner four lines from the lower part of the back of the head ; the portion of them which projected beyond the ordinary plumage were of a white colour."

The bill, which is two inches and three-quarters long, and straight, the lower mandible about a tenth of an inch shorter than the upper one, is of a light brown, much darker at the point ; reddish at the base. Irides, nearly black ; top of head, brown black, mottled with pale yellow brown, and having a central streak of yellow brown running from the forehead to the nape. From each nostril, running backwards over the eye, is a broad stripe of yellow brown ; and extending from the eye to the gape is a streak of brown. Cheeks, yellow brown, mottled with darker brown ; under each eye is a crescentic band of brown, the convexity upwards ; chin and upper throat, brownish or yellowish white. Back and sides of neck, light yellowish brown, mottled with darker brown from the centre of each feather being dark ; centre of back rich black, slightly mottled with light yellow brown ; lower back, generally covered by the long tertials, is brownish black, each feather edged with white. Scapulars and long tertials are black, broadly edged with distinct light yellow brown—forming two light lines down the back from the shoulders ; lower neck and breast, greyish brown, each feather with a darker spot in the centre ; lower breast, abdomen, and vent, pure white ; primaries, brown black. The tail, which consists of fourteen feathers, is black, having a broad band of bright ferruginous colour extending across the tip, in the two centre feathers about half an inch wide, but gradually increasing to the sides, when it is nearly an inch in width; the extreme tips are paler, and inside this is a narrow black band running across all the feathers; the outer feathers are also mottled with ferruginous. Upper tail coverts, light reddish or yellowish brown, narrowly barred with black in zigzag lines. Legs and feet, greenish grey.

The weight of the Snipe is from four to five ounces, but if very fat it will occasionally exceed this weight.

Extreme length, eleven inches and one-third. Expanse of wings, seventeen inches.

The above description is taken from a fine specimen shot near York, just at the commencement of the breeding-season.

As an article of food it is so well known and esteemed that it is hardly necessary to remark upon it. It is dressed on a toast with the trail left in.

BIBLIOGRAPHY.

Sir R. PAYNE-GALLWEY's "Fowler in Ireland" contains an account of its former abundance in that country, and a graphic description of its pursuit and capture by various means.

Messrs. D'URBAN and MATHEW, in "The Birds of Devon," give a very pleasant account of the pursuit of the Snipe in that country.

BOOTH's "Rough Notes" furnish a very full and interesting account of the incidents occurring in Snipe-shooting.

END OF VOL. I.

Printed by BALLANTYNE, HANSON & CO.
Edinburgh and London